EAT TO HEAL

Debbi Nathan &
Helen Nathan

EAT TO HEAL

Over 65 simple, stress-free recipes to supercharge
your health and reduce inflammation and disease

Published by Thread in 2022

An imprint of Storyfire Ltd.
Carmelite House
50 Victoria Embankment
London EC4Y 0DZ

www.thread-books.com

Copyright © Debbi Nathan and Helen Nathan, 2020, 2022

Debbi Nathan and Helen Nathan have asserted their rights
to be identified as the authors of this work.

Food photography by Hannah Bond.
Food photography on pages 114 and 147 Shutterstock images.
Food photography on pages 92, 127, 149 and 152 Freepik.com images.

All rights reserved. No part of this publication may be
reproduced, stored in any retrieval system, or transmitted,
in any form or by any means, electronic, mechanical,
photocopying, recording or otherwise, without the prior written
permission of the publishers.

ISBN: 978-1-83888-995-1
eBook ISBN: 978-1-83888-994-4

Previously published as *Cooking for Your Genes*.

The information herein is not intended to replace the services of trained health and fitness professionals, or be a substitute for medical advice. You are advised to consult with your health care professional with regards to matters relating to your health, and in particular regarding matters that may require diagnosis or medical attention before embarking on a new diet regime.

This book is dedicated to the memory of Grant Fineberg, a unique and wonderful man who left us suddenly at the age of 30, while we were writing this book.

'Do not stand at my grave and cry, I am not there; I did not die.' (Mary Elizabeth Frye)

I love you forever and miss you always, Mom.

To my nephew Grant. Taken too soon, missed by so many. May you be sitting in heaven in a wonderful gingerbread house waiting for us all. Helen

CONTENTS

Foreword 11
Our Story... 12
Introduction 13

Chapter 1: Genes at Work 27
Your Healing Kitchen (by Helen) 31

Chapter 2: Inflammation 35
Your Healing Kitchen 45

BREAKFAST
Baked cinnamon apples 48
Melon, ginger and chia seed fruit salad 49

MAIN MEALS
Butternut squash, pear and leek soup 51
Pan-fried mackerel and capers with rhubarb-and-ginger salsa 52
Baked salmon with caper salsa verde 54
Southern polenta-and-flaxseed
    chicken wings 55
Baked Parmesan courgette fries 56
Soba noodle, tofu and vegetable salad with miso dressing 57

SNACKS AND TREATS
Guacamole 59
Flourless dark chocolate cake with red berry coulis 60

Red berry coulis 61
Turmeric and ginger cookies 62

DRINKS

Strawberry and basil lemonade 64
Pomegranate slushy 65

Chapter 3: Oxidative Stress 66
Your Healing Kitchen 71

BREAKFAST

Super-speedy-no-kneady-seedy bread 75
Garlic mushrooms 76

MAIN MEALS

Pearl barley and porcini mushroom broth 78
Chicken, spinach and lentil saag 79
Allspice red cabbage braised with apples and maple syrup 80
Caponata (Italian ratatouille) 81
Roasted cauliflower, pomegranate and quinoa salad in a jar 82
Spicy Sichuan ginger prawns 83
Chicken satay with spicy peanut dipping sauce 84
Asparagus roasted with garlic and sesame seeds 85
Black bean chocolate chilli 86
Spicy mango guacamole 87
Beetroot tzatziki 88
Brazil nut and tarragon pesto 89
Mexican quinoa salad with orange and lime dressing 90

DRINKS

Chocolate, banana and peanut milkshake 93
Cashew nut and cinnamon milk 94

Chapter 4: Detoxification 95
Your Healing Kitchen 100

BREAKFAST

Spinach, salmon and feta hot cakes 103
Rainbow fruit platter with yogurt and honey 104
Overnight spiced apple oats 105

MAIN MEALS

SPA (spinach, prawn and avocado) salad 107
Blackened miso and ginger marinated cod
  with steamed spinach 108
Debbi's raw broccoli, avocado, feta and mint salad 109
Garlic roasted chicken 111
Broccoli and miso mustard dressing 112
Aloo-gobi (cauliflower, turmeric, pea and onion curry) 113
Wasabi-crusted cod 114
Apple and lemon coleslaw 115
Speedy mayonnaise 116
Sauerkraut 117
Stuffed feta, walnut and parsley roast onions
  with a simple green salad 119
Roast cauliflower nuggets with green chilli pesto 121
Spicy sea bass with a crispy skin 122
Creamy sprout and leek colcannon with pan-fried calf's liver 124

TREATS

Spiced Earl Grey tea loaf 126

DRINKS

Mexican chilli hot chocolate 128
Mo-tea-to mocktail 129
Green smoothie 130

Chapter 5: Methylation 131

Your Healing Kitchen 135

BREAKFAST

Orange and date fruit salad 138
Superberry smoothie 138
Middle Eastern breakfast bowl 139

MAIN MEALS

Easy watercress and spinach soup 141
Pearl barley, feta, parsley and cashew nut salad 141
Broccoli and sweet potato curried fritters 143
Star anise slow-cooked beef ribs 144
Sesame spinach 145
Japanese baked salmon with brown rice and edamame 146
Shakshuka 147

SNACKS

Pea and mint dip 150
Baked beetroot crisps 150
Kale crisps 151

DRINKS

Mango and orange lassi 153
Celery, apple, mint and kiwi summer smoothie 154

References and Further Reading 155
A Note from Debbi and Helen 161
Glossary 162
Acknowledgements 166

Foreword

I first met Debbi Nathan at a DNAlysis Biotechnology training seminar in 2010, where she was introduced to the world of nutrigenomics. The idea that our food and environment choices can have a bearing on our health is not new, with studies to this effect dating back to at least the time of Socrates.

The field of nutrigenomics was accelerated by the draft publishing of the Human Genome Project, and the rapid advances in our understanding of the relationship between genes, nutrition and disease. Most notably, the understanding that the nutrients in our diet can go a long way towards controlling the manner in which our genes express themselves. Thus the historical belief that our genes are our destiny and we need to 'work with the cards we were dealt' has been replaced by the understanding that we are genuinely empowered to control many of our own health outcomes through the diet and lifestyle choices we make during the course of our lives.

Eat to Heal encompasses a global trend and is a must-have for individuals wanting to take more responsibility for their health, where the focus is on prevention rather than cure – identifying risk factors and getting actionable insights to reduce the risk of disease.

There is no more practical and relevant way of utilizing genetics knowledge than to get into a kitchen and cook according to your genes, and Helen's simple, healthy and delicious recipes are the perfect accompaniment to Debbi's compelling explanation of the science behind genetic eating.

Dr Danny Meyersfeld,
PhD Molecular Biology,
CEO and Founder DNAlysis Biotechnology, Director: DNALIFE

Our Story...

Helen and Debbi are sisters-in-law who began their gene journey together over a telephone call as Debbi was preparing to move her life from South Africa to London.

No matter what the conversation is about, they tend to gravitate towards their shared love of food. Debbi is a firm believer in 'you're not too old, and it's not too late', including to take control of your health and reset your body by eating foods to heal, not harm.

As a trained chef, cookery school owner and passionate foodie, Helen knew there was a way to combine their skills and passion. After all, she'd been creating recipes from her London kitchen for over 25 years.

Helen and Debbi decided to combine their talents and marry cutting-edge science with the love of simple, delicious food in order to give people the information they need to make the right choices about what food they should eat.

Before Debbi moved to London in 2017, she worked as a nutritional therapist with a special interest in sports nutrition. 'I am passionate about sharing evidence-based science with my clients so that they can feel better, function better and look better,' she says.

Helen has appeared on national TV and radio, lectured in schools and travelled the world exploring different cuisines. Her passion is teaching people how to make simple, delicious food. She says, 'I hate bland, boring or badly created recipes that lack flavour and take too long to prepare. My mantra is "simple, fresh, fast, delicious and nutritious".'

We hope this book will become a valuable 'food bible'. However, if you decide just to dip in and enjoy the information and cook some of the healthy recipes, you won't be disappointed.

Welcome to *Eat to Heal*!

Helen and Debbi

Introduction

Eat to heal

Are you living your fullest life or being dragged down by fatigue, weight gain, aching joints, lack of energy, or chronic inflammatory disorders? Eating to optimise health and vitality does not have to be punishing.

Nutrition and our eating behaviour have the ability to affect our current health and energy levels as well as predict our future outlook. We can use food to correct some simple inborn 'mishaps' and to try to steer clear of potential ill health.

Prevention is always better than cure. Be empowered and take control of your future by understanding why certain foods are 'good for you' and how they affect you on a cellular level and therefore impact your energy and health. The various chapters in this book demystify and define biological areas such as DETOXIFICATION, INFLAMMATION, OXIDATIVE STRESS and METHYLATION. Although these are different reactions, it's important to understand that they are all dependent on the functionalities of each other. Inflammation and oxidative stress are co-dependent cycles, and nothing exists in a vacuum in our complex and wonderful bodies.

NUTRIGENOMICS is the scientific discipline that studies the interaction between diet, genes and health. This research looks at how foods and specific nutrients affect an individual's genetic make-up, and in return how variations in genes affect the way we react to nutrients in food. Nutrigenomics can help you understand whether your gene variants make you lactose intolerant or predispose you to type 2 diabetes, heart disease or cancer risk.

EPIGENETICS can be thought of as an add-on to the DNA we are born with. Think of epigenetics meaning 'on top of genes'. These additional instructions are responsive to the environment to which an individual is exposed. This environment can include many aspects of human life such as stress, emotions, exercise, nutrition, infection, pollution, extremes in temperature and even how we cook our food. Environmental and dietary factors or gut microbiota can influence foetal, childhood and adult development via epigenetic programming.

Food is information

Put very simply, our genes receive information from the nutrients in food and then translate that into a protein that is used by our cells to function metabolically. The genes themselves do not decide the function of the cell; instead they carry the information or blueprint that is needed to assemble the proteins that actually confer structure and function. This vastly simplified description is called 'gene expression'. This effect is far-reaching, and evidence supports the hypothesis that our early life environment, including nutrition, may impact our future risk for disease.

The recipes in the following chapters all provide vital nutrients that multitask to keep your cell biology working. Many of the recipes are suitable for more than one genetic profile, so a recipe recommended for inflammation may also be recommended for detoxification and oxidative stress. This is because nutrients such as magnesium, zinc and vitamin C do not perform one simple job, but rather they multitask in the world of Systems Biology. These systems and your genes are what make us who we are.

Make food work for you, not against you

There has been a paradigm shift in thinking, and clinical studies clearly show associations between gene variants, nutrition and disease risk.

The concept of 'one size fits all' is no longer relevant in this era of personalization. Family members sitting down together and enjoying the same meal will all respond in different ways once the food is broken down into chemicals and transported through their totally individual biological systems. We differ internally from each other, starting with our gut microbes (billions of bacteria and viruses), as well as our personal responses to inflammation, oxidative stress, detoxification and methylation.

We are indeed unique, and even though we are all expected to function in the same biological way, we differ in how we produce enzymes as well as in how we metabolize nutrients once they enter our systems.

The world is obsessed with health and 'clean' eating, and yet chronic diseases and obesity remain problematic. Pollution, toxins and plastics are choking our cities and oceans. Chronic inflammation and personal stress impact our daily lives and our brilliant bodies, and incredible cellular processes do not always have the capacity to keep up with the continual onslaught. We need to find a balance between twenty-first century living and eating to heal, not harm. By using specific nutrients, we may help to reduce inflammation, support liver detoxification, and protect ourselves from exposure to the toxic load we face daily.

DNA terminology
Unfamiliar terminology can be off-putting, but if molecular biology is not your background, please don't be deterred! We would hate for you to not become involved and excited by this cutting-edge approach to nutrition and wellness, so here are some simple explanations to help you navigate your future health.

DNA
DNA (deoxyribonucleic acid) is where all our hereditary material is stored. The information is stored in the form of a code comprising of base pairs of letters with A (adenine) pairing with T (thymine) and G (guanine) pairing with C (cytosine). These letters form sentences, and each sentence is a gene that carries out instructions for making proteins that determine how our bodies function.

Gene variation and gene mutation
GENE VARIATION is what makes one person less efficient at producing certain enzymes and another person able to produce completely efficient enzymes. This can be seen in the way individuals metabolize folate (vitamin B9, found in leafy greens). Certain people will be more capable of metabolizing and absorbing certain vitamins and minerals due to their genetic make-up. A person with lower enzyme function in their MTHFR gene would need to bump up their intake of leafy greens in order to provide adequate vitamin B9 (folate) which is needed for multiple cellular functions.

We all differ genetically and this is apparent when it comes to caffeine metabolism, lactose intolerance and gluten intolerance. Variations in the CYP1A2 enzyme function results in 'fast' or 'slow' metabolisers of caffeine. If you find you are jittery and wired after drinking coffee, you are most likely a 'slow' metaboliser and should reduce your intake of caffeine. Genes for gluten and lactose will also determine whether or not you have the enzyme capability to metabolise gluten or milk effectively. Side effects are more pronounced in these cases and it's not just a question of cutting back on bread or milk. Bloating, diarrhea, painful joints and brain fog are often related to gluten or lactose intolerance.

GENE MUTATION is a permanent alteration in the DNA sequence that makes up a gene. Mutations can affect gene function in various ways. The mutation can have almost no effect on the functioning of the gene, or it can alter the level of the enzyme that the gene is producing and even prevent the gene from functioning altogether.

Examples of gene mutations that result in a genetic disorder are cystic fibrosis and sickle cell anaemia.

Biomarkers
A biomarker is a traceable substance within blood, urine or tissue, which can be used to identify certain chemicals or signs of disease or infection.

Biomarkers are useful for tracing and tracking nutrients and amino acids and are used to monitor the biological status of an individual. They are a useful tool for measuring how much progress you are making and whether the changes in your diet or supplements are doing the trick or may need further tweaking.

Nutrigenomics
Genetics and nutrition interact. Nutrigenomics is the scientific study of the effect that specific nutrients (food) and nutraceuticals (supplements) have on our inherited genes. Your genes are your inheritance, not your destiny. Nutrigenomics research looks at how foods and specific nutrients affect an individual's genetic make-up and, in turn, how variations in genes (polymorphisms) affect the way individuals react to nutrients in food.

Bioactive ingredients
Bioactive ingredients are found in small amounts in certain plant foods. They can activate gene expression and are important in preventing cancer and other chronic diseases.

Examples of bioactive compounds include: EGCG (epigallocatechin gallate found in green tea), curcumin (derived from turmeric), punicalagin (derived from pomegranate), ascorbate (vitamin C), resveratrol (derived from purple grapes), sulphoraphane (derived from broccoli).

Macros and micros: what are they?
MACRONUTRIENTS are protein, carbohydrates and fats.

MICRONUTRIENTS are vitamins, minerals and antioxidants.

When it comes to nutrients, whether they are macronutrients or micronutrients, please imagine the glorious synergy of an orchestra. Each instrument and musician plays their role and sometimes they have a solo, but it's all in context of the bigger picture and the overall affect it has on the audience. In this case the audience is your body. *Eat to Heal* is aimed at helping you to acknowledge how special we all are and how best to achieve optimal health within the framework of your body, using food to compose a symphony.

The main players are of course the macronutrients that provide the basic fuel necessary to produce energy. We need them to get through the day without running out of steam. Both under-nourishment and over-nourishment create huge problems for health and wellness. So, let's set the stage for the ideal 'Goldilocks' scenario. Not too little, not too much – just right.

Out inherited genetics play a major role in determining how we metabolise carbohydrates, fats, and proteins as well as our satiety (hunger) hormones. At the same time, we are overwhelmed with arguments exposing the 'horrors' of carbohydrates, protein and of course, fat. In *Eat to Heal*, neither are the enemy. The enemy that stands in the way of optimal health is indeed overly processed, chemically enhanced foods.

The modern Western diet, which is low in fibre, high in processed fats and carbohydrates, with excessive consumption of sugar, and chemically enhanced flavourings, is designed to tip the balance in favour of ill health. We will probably have to look more closely at future food labels as the market explodes with plant-based alternatives, which may also be drowned in processed chemicals and fake food!

Protein

The biggest decision you will make today could be at the end of your fork. Protein is literally at the top of the food chain and essential for survival.

Whether you are a carnivore, paleo, pescatarian, vegan, vegetarian or a Veganuary person, protein is essential, and is often associated purely with muscle building. But there is so much more to this! It's needed to make new cells, neurotransmitters (brain chemicals), enzymes, hormones, and all muscle cells including heart cells.

If you're eating to heal, then amino acids, the 'building blocks' of protein, are essential to almost all biological pathways. There is more to come on these pathways in chapters focussed on detoxification, inflammation, oxidative stress and methylation.

But what is protein, besides a chicken breast?

Protein is a construction of 20 amino acids, which are the building blocks. Nine of these amino acids are essential, which means we need to get them from our diet, and the remaining eleven can be made by our bodies. Our DNA provides instructions for making proteins which are formed using different combinations of amino acids. This is how a skin cell knows how to become a skin cell and a muscle cell knows how to become a muscle cell and what gives rise to the enormous variability in humans, from our eye and hair colour to our ability to manage our health.

Protein builds muscle and athletes generally require higher amounts of protein to enhance muscle growth and repair cells. Not all of us are high performing athletes, but exercise should be an essential component in our daily lives. Apart from repairing muscle, protein is needed to maintain skin, hair, bone, teeth, tendons and ligaments and internal organs. The vital amino acids that make up proteins, as well as vitamins and minerals in protein sources, are important for supporting pathways that impact mental health and optimal cognitive function

Ideally, protein should be consumed at all meals as it helps to balance blood sugar levels and keeps us feeling fuller for longer, reducing the urge to snack on sugary stuff.

For the non-athletic population, getting about 1.0 to 1.2 grams per kilogram per day is recommended. That means if you are a man weighing 75 kg, you would ideally need to consume 75–90 grams of protein per day. A woman weighing 60 kg would require approximately 60 grams of protein per day.

As stated previously, this requirement would be higher for an athlete, but kidney function will also play a major role in protein synthesis and requirements. Above-average intakes of protein may place a strain on the kidneys.

Animal protein is generally the most complete source of protein and contains all the essential amino acids. Our genetics also determine to a large extent who will thrive on higher protein and fats and who will manage well with a vegan diet.

An average serving of animal protein is 20 g and this can be obtained from a variety and combination of plant and animal protein sources in meals and snacks.

The highest source of bioavailable protein (protein that is absorbed) is high-quality whey protein. Next on the list in order of protein content is the humble egg. After that comes chicken. In this case, the egg comes before the chicken, followed in turn by turkey, casein, fish, lean meat, and milk.

Vegan protein is a trickier issue due to an incomplete amino acid profile. However, quinoa, soya beans, buckwheat, chia, and spirulina have proven to be great sources of protein for vegan and vegetarian diets.

Other sources of vegan protein that remain incomplete in amino acids are rice, wheat, nuts, seeds, peanuts, barley, corn, chickpeas, peas, and beans.

By combining various sources of plant and/or animal proteins throughout the day, it's not that difficult to maintain the optimal amounts to keep your body functioning at its best.

Carbohydrates: 'one man's meat, another man's poison'
By 1980, fat was declared the enemy in mainstream diets, and low fat was the 'only way' to go. This has now been turned on its head and the current

target is carbohydrates. There is no 'one size fits all' and what may work like magic for some people will create havoc in others. It's all very confusing!

The clear facts are that highly processed carbohydrates available in supermarket snack aisles, and fast-food outlets, are bad for us. Consuming doughnuts, processed cereals, biscuits, chips, crisps, and pizza regularly results in metabolic chaos. If it comes out of a packet and has a long, unreadable list of 'ingredients', it's generally not going to help you heal. In fact, it is probably harmful.

But there are a host of 'good guys' waiting to be scooped into your trolley, and turned into delicious, nourishing, healing foods. Look no further – we have a pile of recipes to prove it!

The difference between LOW GI (glycaemic index) carbohydrates, HIGH GI carbohydrates and the GL (glycaemic load) is all about insulin.

The hormone insulin is a key regulator of energy metabolism, and is one of the fundamental hormones that promotes fat accumulation and storage. Insulin is a storage hormone. When we eat, insulin is released and what cannot be used by the cells as energy is stored as glycogen and fat. When the demand on insulin is consistently high the cells become insulin resistant, an inflammatory condition which, left unchecked, becomes type 2 diabetes.

The digestive system breaks down carbohydrates, converts them into glucose and transports it into our bloodstream. The pancreas secretes the hormone insulin which helps move glucose from our bloodstream into our cells. Once inside the cells, glucose is 'burned' with oxygen to produce energy. Our brain, muscles, and nervous system all rely on this precious fuel to produce energy all day long.

Carbohydrates that are broken down quickly during digestion have a higher GI, and carbohydrates that are broken down slowly have a lower GI.

The GLYCAEMIC INDEX of food is defined as the time it takes for glucose to appear in your bloodstream. The more highly processed the food, the higher the GI. The GI (glycaemic index) of a food or meal and the overall impact on an individual is influenced by factors such as the type of sugar it contains, as well as the cooking method and your genetic profile.

The GL (glycaemic load) is measured by the type and quality of carbohydrates you eat. Eating a balanced meal of lean protein, low-GI green and yellow vegetables and brown rice will have both a low GI and low GL.

Gluten intolerance

Gluten is a protein found in certain grains such as wheat, barley, rye, and spelt. The gliadin in protein is what generally causes stomach irritation. Mild gluten intolerance differs to serious intolerances such as Crohn's disease, inflammatory bowel disease, or Coeliac disease, which have genetic components.

Undigested gluten proteins are used by enzymes (transglutaminase), which allows the gluten to attach to DQ2.2 cells. This group is then presented to the CD4 + T cells of the immune system which results in an inflammatory response, causing potential intestinal tissue damage.

Gluten intolerance can increase with age as we become more prone to inflammation and our gut barrier function weakens.

Milder symptoms include bloating, flatulence, post-nasal drip, lung irritation, and skin conditions.

Severe gastrointestinal symptoms are cramps, diarrhea and constipation, as well as joint pain, asthma, eczema, chronic fatigue, depression, and brain fog.

The following foods should be avoided in a gluten-free diet:

- Wheat (including bulgar)
- Wholewheat flour
- White flour
- Rye
- Spelt
- Barley
- Durum flour

- Triticale
- Oats (if very sensitive)
- Thickening agents in gravy and sauces

The following foods are gluten free:

- Buckwheat
- Quinoa
- Amaranth
- Rice – white/brown/wild rice
- Corn/maize
- Legumes
- Mesquite
- Millet
- Nuts
- Seeds
- Potatoes
- Sweet potato
- Polenta
- Tapioca
- Sorghum
- Gluten-free oats

Fats: the good, the bad and the truly ugly

If it's made in a factory, it's probably truly ugly. TRANS-FATS are made using high heat and pressure to add hydrogen molecules to vegetable oils. They are highly inflammatory and a risk for heart disease, strokes, type 2 diabetes, Alzheimer's disease and cancer. Check for food labels that contain 'mono- and diglycerides of fatty acids' and avoid:

- Margarines
- Hydrogenated vegetable oils
- Re-used oils
- Oils heated at high temperatures

Fat is an essential nutrient and is vital for brain function, cell membranes, nerve function, producing sex hormones, and providing energy. The type and amount of fat in our diets is very individual and dependent on our genes. Some people thrive on a high-fat diet while others don't.

The really good fats that we all need to include in our diets are omega-3 fats that come from raw nuts, raw seeds, cold-pressed virgin olive oil, cold processed hemp oil, or algae or seaweed. Oily fish such as salmon, mackerel, herring and tuna contain higher levels, but all fish contain omega-3 fats. Egg yolk also contains omega-3 fats.

Let's not forget about omega-6 fats. These are essential to include but should be consumed at a lower ratio to omega-3s. A higher ratio of omega-6 fats can be inflammatory in some people. Try to source free-range, grass-fed meat and free-range chicken and eggs wherever possible. Good sources of omega-6 are Brazil nuts, sesame seeds, walnuts, avocadoes, pumpkin seeds, flax seeds, evening primrose oil and blackcurrant oils.

Antioxidants

The term antioxidants encompasses a vast array of internal enzymes and genes as well as edible plant-based common foods.

The delicate balance between oxidants such as free radicals, cigarette smoke, pollutants and chemicals, which result in oxidative damage, and the knights in shining armour, called antioxidants, is kept in check by our bodies own built-in (endogenous) antioxidant defence system. The human body produces metabolic antioxidants such melatonin, amino acids, and other essential elements that fuel our cells to protect us and produce energy. However, we also rely heavily on obtaining antioxidants such as vitamin E, vitamin C, carotenoids, flavonoids, omega-3 and omega-6 fatty acids as well as trace minerals (zinc, selenium, manganese) from our daily food intake. To support our internal antioxidant system, we should be eating a variety of colourful antioxidants derived from plant foods or supplements, if necessary.

Some common examples of antioxidant-rich foods are broccoli, spinach, kale, parsley, kiwi fruit, garlic, onions, grapes, berries, cherries, watermelon, dark chocolate, apples, peaches, pomegranate, pink grapefruit, black tea, green tea, pumpkin, mango, papaya, carrots, apricots, sweet potatoes, tomatoes, red and yellow peppers, corn, oranges, artichokes and lentils.

Zinc and selenium are found in seafood, lean meats, offal, wholegrains and nuts.

Manganese is found in seafood, oats, bran, dark chocolate, almonds, pecans, brown rice, lima beans and pinto beans.

Antioxidants are a large family of chemicals, called phytochemicals. As the word 'phyto' suggests, these nutrients are found in plants. Many of these nutrients are bioactive compounds. This means that they have been shown scientifically to be able to activate gene expression. For example, EGCG is a bioactive compound found in green tea that can help reduce oxidative stress and fight inflammation. Other antioxidants such as ginger, curcumin (turmeric), and resveratrol found in red grapes and even peanuts are also bioactive compounds and provide antioxidant protection.

We all know broccoli is good for us, but it's the sulphoraphane in broccoli that is the bioactive ingredient that activates genes to 'step into the ring' and neutralise the enemy.

Fabulous phytochemicals – food as a tool for the prevention of illness

Over the last few decades we have learnt that food is far more than just basic carbohydrates, proteins and fats. This new awareness has opened the door to further research and a growth in public interest in the benefits of plant food.

Phytochemicals are biologically active compounds, which means they have antioxidant capabilities and can also impact DNA repair. Interestingly, many phytochemicals that are good for us also produce bright colours in fruit and vegetables and that is where the saying 'eat the rainbow' comes from (see Table 0.1).

Table 0.1: Phytochemicals/antioxidants in foods

Colours	Food examples	Protective antioxidant compounds
Red	Tomato, strawberry, cranberry, watermelon, wild salmon, prawns, peppers	Lycopene, astaxanthin, anthocyanins, vitamin C
Orange	Carrot, yam, sweet potato, pumpkin, mango, apricot, turmeric	Beta-carotene, curcumin, vitamin A, vitamin C
Yellow-orange	Orange, lemon, grapefruit, papaya, peach, melon, egg yolk, sweetcorn, pineapple	Lutein, flavanones, vitamin C, vitamin A, vitamin E
Green-white	Broccoli, spinach, kale, Brussels sprouts, cabbage, cauliflower, lettuce, cucumber, garlic, onions, leeks, celery, watercress	Multiple antioxidants, e.g. sulphoraphane, allicin, quercetin, ferulic acid, caffeic acid, vitamin K, vitamin C, vitamin A
Blue	Blueberries, purple grapes, plums	Anthocyanins, pycnogenol, vitamin C
Red-purple	Grapes, berries, plums, prunes, raisins, raspberries, red cabbage, beetroot/beet, aubergine/eggplant, purple potatoes, purple carrots	Resveratrol, pycnogenol, anthocyanins, proanthocyanidins, vitamin C
Brown	Wholegrains, legumes, 85% dark chocolate, nuts, seeds	Fibre to aid detoxification, vitamin E, flavonols, anthocyanins, magnesium, copper

More and more compelling evidence reveals that it is not the act of one single compound that 'gets the job done' but the synergy of a variety of phytochemicals with their fibre intact and various vitamins and minerals that all combine to provide the cell protection we need to fight chronic disease.

At present, about 6,000 different polyphenols have been found in plant foods and many have become quite familiar to us. For example, curcumin (the yellow colour in turmeric) and resveratrol (in red grapes and red wine), sulphoraphane (in broccoli and Brussels sprouts) and EGCG (in green tea).

It's important to include a wide variety of different plant foods in your diet. Each of the many foods rich in phytochemicals (polyphenols, antioxidants, anthocyanins, flavonols, carotenoids, terpenoids) can support many different reactions in our cells.

Chapter 1

Genes at Work

Information is power. All the information about yourself is stored and coded in your DNA, which is, in turn, housed in your genes.

Your genes are responsible for making proteins. Each gene has instructions to make a specific protein, and these proteins become chemical messengers (mRNA) carrying instructions to your cells for example, whether a cell is to become a skin cell or a liver cell, the colour of your eyes and skin, etc. Although humans have many similar features, unique differences determine who 'you' are.

In order to perform their essential job of making proteins, genes need to be activated. Activation requires contacting a specific gene to produce its specific protein to deliver the right message. Sounds simple? Considering there are about 24,000 genes in the human genome, some of which have functions we cannot explain, that leaves a lot of room for error. The remarkable human body has precautions in place, and the focus in nutrigenomics is on upstream processes like detoxification to remove harmful toxins and the process of reducing oxidative stress (the balance between pro-oxidants and antioxidants) in our cells. The human body is a complex, interconnected system that results in domino-type effects of biological and chemical processes. No system is isolated – what happens in the gut, liver, brain, muscles or heart all have an impact on each other. There are four main upstream processes – detoxification, inflammation, oxidative stress and energy production within our cells. An inflammatory process upstream or gene expression upstream will impact other processes further along the route.

The human body has remarkable defence systems
Diet and lifestyle play a major role in supporting the defence systems that guard our cells. Some of us have better defence systems than others,

and there are also genetic 'outliers' who appear luckier than others. For example, my grandfather smoked 60 cigarettes a day and polished off my grandmother's superb cheesecake on a weekly basis. He was never hospitalized and died peacefully in his sleep at 85 years old without any aches or pains in his overweight body. By contrast, what should we make of a fit young man tragically dying mid-marathon from sudden cardiac death? Undetected existing cardiovascular disease or genetic risks had little to do with his physical conditioning and he 'appeared' perfectly healthy to those around him, unlike my grandfather who looked as though he may expire from a coughing fit at any moment.

Is it simply a case of having 'good genes' or is there more to this?

Our internal defence systems work tirelessly to keep us functioning, but they also need a bit of support from ourselves. During World War 1, soldiers whose diets contained garlic had less frequent bouts of dysentery than those who did not eat garlic.

Going back a bit further, nearly 2,000 years ago, ancient Greek physicians were using garlic as a 'superfood'. Garlic contains allicin, which is a potent antioxidant for scavenging free radicals. Free radicals are also known as reactive oxygen species or pro-oxidants. Garlic has been used for centuries as an antibacterial and anti-viral compound. Garlic and garlic juice have also been shown to inhibit Helicobacter pylori, the bacteria responsible for stomach ulcer formation. There are so many reasons to add the ancient, delicious ingredient to our recipes!

Another simple ingredient to include in your medicinal recipe collection is cranberry juice. Cranberry juice has been used for years by women suffering with urinary tract infections. Scientists have now proved that 300 ml/10½ fl oz cranberry juice per day, taken for six months, can alter bacterial flora in the urinary tract. Foods and nutrients that are capable of modulating gene expression are called 'bioactive compounds'.

It's important to note that "our genes load the gun, but environment pulls the trigger'. We cannot alter the genes we were born with, BUT we can certainly manipulate our health outcome using nutrition, exercise and healthy choices as the tools. Let's pause for a minute to look at some terminology.

GENE EXPRESSION or gene regulation is the process by which the information in our genes is translated into proteins. Genes have a coding area that contains all the instructions for making the proteins. Gene expression is the result of how much or how little of the information is passed along. Think of a dimmer switch on the wall controlling how much light gets into the room. These proteins act as 'workers', delivering these decoded instructions to our cells and letting them know what function to perform. Gene expression is the result of how much of the information gets through. One of the triggers for altering the 'dimmer switch' is nutrition.

The food we eat on a daily basis affects our gene expression by either accelerating or slowing down the action of a particular gene and causing the genes to produce smaller or greater amounts of various proteins which, in turn, affects how our bodies function.

OXIDATIVE STRESS is an everyday cellular process. Normal everyday metabolism requires our cells to use oxygen to produce energy. The by-product of this everyday process produces *free radicals*.

Free radicals are also known as reactive oxygen species (ROS), or pro-oxidants. A delicate balance between free radicals and antioxidants needs to be maintained in our cells to keep us healthy. This balance can be difficult to maintain when we are exposed to excessive cigarette smoke, pollution, chemicals, chronic life stressors and overtraining syndrome in athletes.

When there is an imbalance or overwhelm of these systems, oxidative damage to cells occurs and contributes to human diseases such as cancer, neurological disorders, cardiovascular diseases, diabetes, and pulmonary disease.

High levels of oxidative stress can also contribute to accelerated ageing of the skin and is visible in the form of wrinkles and prematurely aged skin.

BIOACTIVE ingredients are found in small amounts in certain fruits, vegetables, grains, nuts and oils. Bioactive compounds can activate gene expression and have therefore been studied for their anti-cancer actions.

There are certain bioactive compounds that over-perform once you have eaten them and they can then exert a positive influence by increasing the protective function and vitality of the cells in many more ways than intended. Top of the list are broccoli and fermented vegetables such as kimchi and sauerkraut. Not only are the foods providing essential vitamins and minerals, but the downstream effect is magnified due to the ability to positively impact gene expression. Sulphoraphane in these foods is able to activate the Nrf2 pathway.

The Nrf2 signalling pathway can alter the expression of about 2,000 cytoprotective genes, which can neutralize and detoxify drugs and toxins, protect against oxidative stress and inflammation, and help remove damaged proteins from our bodies. Some scientists believe that this signalling pathways plays an essential role in determining the health and lifespan of our species and may be the regulator of the ageing process.

Including a serving of broccoli and/or naturally fermented kimchi and sauerkraut in your daily diet may be a simple way of improving your overall health.

We all need the same nutrients and vitamins in order to survive and to stay healthy. The science of nutrigenomics focuses on you, the individual, with different amounts of each nutrient needed to make you function optimally. What will it take to make you produce the correct amount of proteins and chemicals to activate your unique gene expression?

One can assume that if there is an issue with certain chronic diseases in the family, you could go ahead and safely follow the recipes recommended for detoxification, inflammation and/or oxidative stress. Chronic disease may possibly be avoided or symptoms alleviated by reducing inflammation and avoiding highly processed foods and chemicals.

Your Healing Kitchen (by Helen)

The recipes throughout this book support all the biological pathways and are created to be used as a daily guide. A recipe that is ideal for methylation will also support an anti-inflammatory diet and this in turn, will support oxidative stress and detoxification pathways as well.

What is a nutrigenomic diet?
We all metabolize food differently due to our very individual gut microbiome as well as our individual biochemistry and the manner in which we produce and use energy. We all, however, strive to achieve optimal health while enjoying great food.

When Debbi first explained the concept of a nutrigenomic diet, my initial concern as a chef was that science might dominate over flavour. I'm not a fan of faddy diets. I love good, wholesome food; warm bowls of soup with crusty bread and a bit of butter, a large Greek salad with a chilled glass of rosé and the occasional slab of chocolate cake. Food to me isn't just fuel, it's family get-togethers, candle-lit dinners, picnics in the park and large raucous parties that go on a little too late because the food tastes great and everyone is having fun. Of course, not every meal is a celebration, but great food doesn't mean slaving over a hot stove. Good food can be quick and easy and shouldn't be a chore.

Was this 'nutrigenomic diet' going to fit with my values and was I going to have to be rigid and only eat foods I know are supposed to be 'good for me'?

The more I discussed the topic with Debbi, the happier I became. It isn't about restriction, but rather teaching people how to use ingredients that work for them. It can still be about celebrating wonderful flavours and creating interesting, tasty food that everyone can enjoy. It's all about *your* DNA and how your internal systems react to specific food.

Each chapter covers a different metabolic area within the body, using nutrients that have been scientifically proven to impact gene expression. This is known as 'epigenetics'.

Epigenetics can be thought of as an add-on to the DNA we are born with. 'Epi' means 'on top of' genes. Our diet, lifestyle, emotions and environment (both external and internal) have a direct impact on how our genes respond. Epigenetics controls genes and is known as gene expression. Gene expression can be compared to a light switch being turned on or off. Certain bioactive foods can activate gene expression in a positive way, and that's the reason why we say 'food talks to your genes'. In certain diseases such as cancer, various genes will be switched on or off, away from the normal healthy state.

Knowing your genetic predisposition allows you to make positive choices to enhance your health, rather than fuel a potential fire.

The word 'diet' makes me shiver slightly. The recipes in this book are not 'diet food'; they are just delicious food that happens to also thankfully be good for you too. Hurray! A win-win! So, the science part comes first in each chapter and then we split the recipes into:

- *Fast food* – This group of foods/menu recommendations can be prepared quickly when you're on the go and when time is not on your side.
- *Easy recipes* – My easy recipes are packed with flavour and are on the whole speedy to prepare. I've included breakfast options, lunches you can pre-make and either freeze or store in the fridge, plus evening meals (both savoury and sweet).

Your Healing Kitchen larder
Below is a 'starter kit' list of ingredients that are known to have positive health benefits and are used extensively in the recipes included in this book. It does not include fruit and vegetables, nor fresh ingredients. Organic is always best if possible. Whenever possible, try to stick to fresh, seasonal produce.

- Dried apricots
- Turmeric
- Cold-pressed olive oil
- Green tea
- All nuts (no added salt or flavourings)
- Dark chocolate
- Pumpkin, sesame, sunflower and flaxseeds
- Quinoa
- Brown rice
- Lentils
- Capers
- Tahini

- Miso
- Pearl barley
- Star anise
- Tamari/soy sauce
- Honey
- Maple syrup
- Cinnamon
- Chia seeds
- Chipotle paste
- Black beans
- Organic porridge oats/rolled oats
- Wasabi paste
- Apple cider vinegar
- Chilli flakes
- Black Darjeeling tea
- Cocoa powder
- Soba noodles
- Polenta

Great gadgets and essential kitchen equipment!

The following small kitchen gadgets will help to make life easier:

- Sharp knives (obvious, I know, but it really does make a difference when preparing food)
- Good set of sturdy pots, pans and frying pans
- Sieve/strainer
- Garlic crusher
- Handheld blender
- Chopping boards (ideally wooden boards to reduce plastic usage)
- Electric whisk
- Loaf tin
- Cake tin/cake pan
- Silicon tray liners (not essential, but extremely helpful!)
- Apple corer
- Cheese grater
- Parchment paper
- Empty jar with lid for shaking salad dressings
- Weighing scales
- Measuring jug/bowl

Great easy salad dressings to store in the fridge

Below is a selection of salad dressings that can multitask. For example, the miso mustard could be used as a marinade for chicken or fish, the Asian dressing can be poured on brown rice to add flavour and interest and the walnut dressing could be added to broccoli or leeks. They are all very simple to make – just put all the ingredients for each recipe in a jar, screw the lid on tightly and shake – and will last up to 2 weeks in the fridge.

Asian salad dressing
Finely grated zest and juice of 1 lime
1 fresh long red chilli, deseeded and finely chopped
1 tsp brown sugar or maple syrup
3 tbsp rapeseed/canola oil
1 garlic clove, crushed

Miso mustard dressing
½ tsp Dijon mustard
2 tbsp miso (white or brown)
1 tbsp clear honey
1½ tbsp rice vinegar
3 tbsp water

Tahini dressing
2 tbsp tahini
1 tbsp lemon juice
1 garlic clove, crushed
2 tbsp water
1 tsp maple syrup

Helen's go-to salad dressing
4 tbsp olive oil
2 tbsp sherry vinegar
1 tbsp maple syrup
good pinch of sea salt

Walnut dressing
1 tbsp walnut oil
2 tbsp rapeseed/canola oil
handful of walnuts, roughly chopped
1 tbsp white wine vinegar
salt and pepper

Japanese 'matsuhisa' dressing
1 small onion, peeled and finely grated
2 tsp soy sauce
1 tsp rice vinegar
2 tsp water
½ tsp granulated sugar
pinch of sea salt
¼ tsp powdered mustard
pinch of freshly ground black pepper
4 tsp grapeseed oil
4 tsp sesame oil

Chapter 2

Inflammation

'Ouch!' is how inflammation sounds. Inflammation mostly brings to mind a red, sore throat, an achy knee or an infected cut. Those common aches are indeed part of the inflammatory process, but the reaction runs far deeper than the skin's surface.

A runaway fire
Not all inflammation is bad – in fact, it's a very necessary and natural response to enable our bodies to fight off foreign invaders and infection. As soon as danger is detected, our immune system signals the inflammatory system and 'fighters' in the form of cytokines and Th-1 cells are sent in to do battle and regulate the human immune response. These chemical messengers are the first responders to an injury and even to high-intensity exercise. This is a signalling mechanism that should facilitate the next steps in the healing and recovery process and is known as *acute inflammation*. Certain individuals are more prone to having a higher inflammatory response and instead of these genes and signalling molecules going back to their quiet corners and waiting to be called upon, they hang around and remain activated. This is a very simplified explanation for a very complex cascade of signalling pathways. That being said, inflammatory disorders and immune system dysregulation has become a common concern and the list of chronic inflammatory disorders is long.

The second type of inflammation is called *chronic inflammation* (see Figure 2.1). The problem with inflammation arises when our inflammatory genes respond to an alarm and then remain in the on position and don't switch off and wait until they are called upon to tackle the next issue. If left unchecked, this lingering response causes

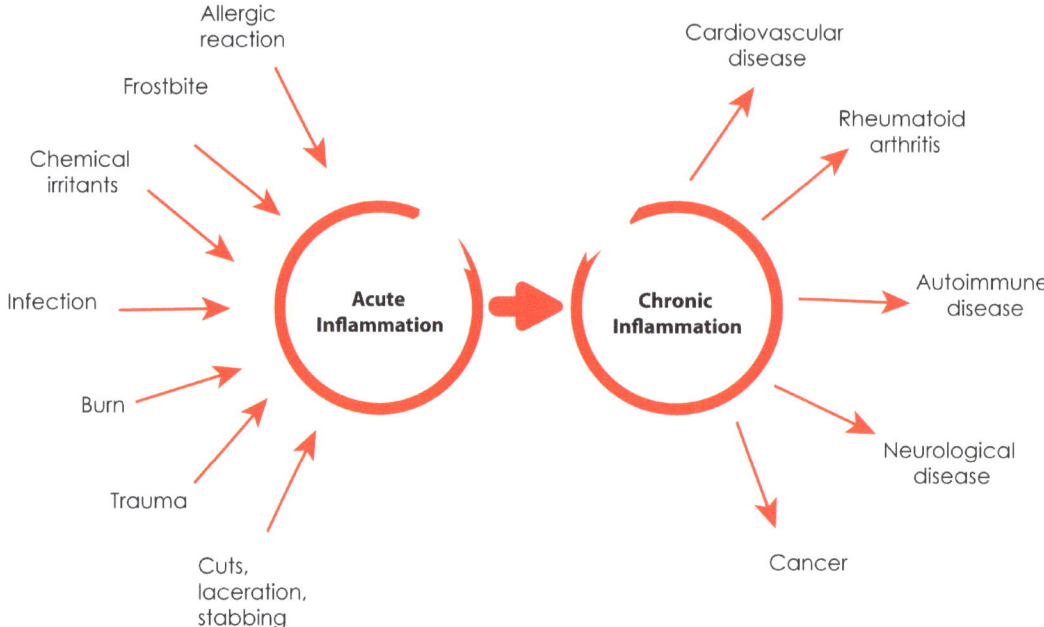

Figure 2.1: Acute and chronic inflammation add fuel to the fire

the immune system to activate white blood cells to attack healthy tissues and organs and may lead to disruptive diseases such as rheumatoid arthritis, cancer, heart disease, diabetes, asthma and Alzheimer's disease.

Inflammation and oxidative stress are co-dependent: one reaction affects the other in an ongoing, self-perpetuating cycle. This is a bit like malware that gets into our hard drive and then disrupts and hacks all the other carefully organized programs.

What drives inflammation?

Inflammation can be driven by genetic predisposition (it runs in the family) or by an immune system that is highly sensitive to environmental factors (for example, pollution, pollen, chemicals and pesticides, cigarette smoke, medication) and therefore elicits a strong histamine (allergic) response. Sometimes it's a combination of factors. Our gastrointestinal tract (digestion) plays a major role in the immune system's inflammatory response.

Chronic low-grade inflammation is linked to almost all major chronic diseases. The continual activation of immune system cells builds up in our tissues, and what was once healthy tissue becomes ravaged by inflammation and then disease. Heart disease, such as atherosclerosis (blocked blood vessels), and type 2 diabetes are now commonly recognized as inflammatory disorders.

Chronic consumption of the modern Western diet – low fibre, processed fats and carbohydrates, and an excessive consumption of sugar – coupled with sedentary behaviour, has given birth to the term 'metaflammation'. This process is mostly driven by lifestyle and learned behaviour. If parents don't follow a healthy active lifestyle, their children will often fall into the same pattern.

Many common conditions that were quite rare a few years ago are linked to CHRONIC INFLAMMATION: obesity, insulin resistance, type 2 diabetes, heart disease, rheumatoid arthritis, asthma, lupus, psoriasis, eczema, thyroid disorders, inflammatory bowel disease, irritable bowel syndrome, osteoporosis, certain cancers, and neurological disorders such as depression and Alzheimer's disease.

Inflammation in the brain
We all have days and moments when we feel 'stressed out of our minds', but serious neurological and neuropsychiatric disorders have strong links to oxidative stress and NEUROINFLAMMATION. Neuroinflammation, or inflammation in our central nervous system, is divided into two types. Acute inflammation occurs as the result of an injury or traumatic incident; chronic inflammation is typically associated with neurodegenerative disorders.

Inflammation in the body applies to the brain as well. Cytokines are molecules that aid cell-to-cell communication in the immune system. The primary function of cytokines is to regulate inflammation. Cytokines are very important for the development of normal brain function and can influence neurocircuitry (brain wiring) and neurotransmitter (chemical brain messenger) systems to adapt to behavioural alterations. Social stress such as divorce/separation, social alienation, past experiences and childhood trauma can all lead to an increase in circulating inflammatory cytokines. Bacterial and viral infections and gut barrier dysfunction can also lead to an increase in inflammatory signalling. Continual exposure to these molecules can lead to mood disorders and cognitive decline (brain ageing).

The human brain is protected by the blood–brain barrier (BBB) a structure that is semi-permeable and forms the barrier between the circulating blood and the brain. This allows some molecules, such as glucose, water and amino acids, to pass through but prevents toxins and pathogens (infections) from crossing into the brain. As in the gut, this barrier function can become faulty due to inflammation.

The brain does not have the same antioxidant defence system as the rest of our organs and is lower in antioxidant activity compared to other organs such as the liver. The brain is one of the busiest organs needed to keep all the other organs functioning properly. The brain needs more oxygen and glucose to make energy and this requirement makes it susceptible to oxygen overload, which results in the release of more free radicals that need to be mopped up. Our hardworking brains are poorly protected from oxidative stress and inflammation, and the links between an unhealthy gut, infections, individual genetics and our diet and lifestyles have a resounding impact on our brain function.

Chronic stress, both physical and emotional, has been shown to increase activation of inflammatory markers as well as a reduced sensitivity to cortisol. Cortisol is a very potent anti-inflammatory hormone, but under conditions of chronic stress, our immune and adrenal system can no longer cope with the amount of cortisol being released and we become glucocorticoid resistant, or 'burnt out'. Instead of this ancient survival system being used only when danger presents itself, many of us remain 'stuck' in that fight–flight mode. Adaptogens have been used for centuries in Chinese and Ayurvedic medicine. Plants and herbs such as ashwagandha, rhodiola, Siberian ginseng, liquorice root and reishi mushroom can all be used effectively to assist the body to adapt to chronic stress.

Inflammation of the gut
Smoking, stress, genetics, allergies, pharmaceuticals, infection, toxins, alcohol, illness, overuse of antibiotics, appendectomy, lack of dietary fibre, processed

foods, ageing, artificial sweeteners and sedentary behaviour (as well as excessive exercise) can all contribute to inflammation in the gut.

We acquire our microbiome at birth, either via the vaginal canal during natural birth, or directly from the midwife or doctors during a caesarean section. The microbiota is fully formed by three years of age. Even though you may have a similar microbiota to other members of your family, it will not be identical. Children growing up on a farm will have completely different microbiota to children or adults living in a city.

A healthy gut means that we have a balance and, most importantly, diversity of all the microbiota that live communally within our gut and body.

The gut barrier covers a surface area of about 400 m^2 and requires about 40% of the body's energy expenditure. This vast and highly complex barrier system must allow fluid and nutrients to pass through to keep us nourished, and yet also protect us from invading micro-organisms. Apart from this physical barrier, a chemical barrier exists, which contains our inflammatory cytokines. This is our body's line of defence against invading and possible harmful organisms.

A thin layer of cells separates the gut barrier from the mucus layer, circulating blood and our microbiota. Under normal, healthy conditions, the mucosal lining and the tight barrier junctions in the gut keep the bacteria and toxins confined to where they should be. Acute or chronic inflammation causes this tightly controlled barrier to lose function and gaps appear in the barrier, allowing microbes to flow into circulating blood and tissue.

The MICROBIOTA are all the microscopic bacteria, viruses and fungi within the human body. This amounts to about 100 trillion bacteria in the intestine.

The MICROBIOME contains all the genes of these microbes. This amounts to 150 times more genes than the entire human genome.

PROBIOTICS are live, friendly microflora that can be taken as a supplement or derived from cultured or fermented foods.

PREBIOTICS are manufactured from dietary fibre and feed and nurture our microbiota.

SHORT-CHAIN FATTY ACIDS (SCFAs) are produced from the breakdown of prebiotics and act as further protection within the gut. SCFAs provide antioxidant and anti-inflammatory protection. Butyrate, which is produced by fermentation of SCFAs, controls human dendritic cell maturation. Dendritic cells are formed in the blood and, as they mature, they migrate to the lymph nodes and act as messengers between the innate and adaptive immune system. They are found mostly in the skin, nose, lungs, mouth, stomach and intestines. Dendritic cells are considered 'gatekeepers' of the immune system.

The GUT–BRAIN AXIS is a bi-directional signalling process between the central nervous system of the brain and the enteric nervous system of the gut. This brings to mind the common phrase 'gut feeling', and most of us have had 'butterflies' in our stomachs when we've felt anxious about something. The mechanisms of the gut-brain axis (GBA) involve neuro-immuno-endocrine system communication. This complex 'cross-talk' between the endocrine system (known as the hypothalamic-pituitary-adrenal axis), the immune system and the autonomic nervous system (ANS) allows the brain to influence intestinal function.

All aspects of this complex system seem to be heavily affected by the signalling activity of the microbiota living in the gut.

This 'cross-talk' between the gut and the brain results in changes in the stress response and overall behaviour of an individual. Chronic stress has been shown to change and affect the protective gut barrier which leads to 'leaky gut syndrome' and has been linked to psychiatric conditions such as depression. Probiotics have often proved successful in treating people with irritable bowel syndrome (IBS) by reducing the anxiety and stress response and lowering the inflammatory cytokine response of the immune system. The stress axis is a key player in the regulation of adrenal hormones, which in turn have a knock-on effect on cortisol, thyroid, oestrogen, and testosterone production. Continual activation of the stress axis results in a blunting of the cortisol response, and as in insulin resistance, the cells stop 'hearing' the normal signals. Chronic stress, whether its emotional and/or physical (due to excessive exercise) increases inflammation, disrupts hormone signalling, and influences blood sugar and unwanted weight gain.

Approximately 95% of serotonin (our 'feel-good' chemical) is produced in the gut, and it relies on 90% of the good bacteria in our gut for its production. Gut microbiota also play a role in the metabolism of tryptophan (a precursor to the production of serotonin).

Changes in serotonin signalling have now been linked to inflammatory bowel disease (IBD) as well as in severe constipation.

Chronic inflammatory immune activity is being linked to many neurological disorders such as Parkinson's disease. The presence of small intestinal bacterial overgrowth (SIBO) has been seen in some Parkinson's disease patients who have been more affected by motor impairment.

Changes in the diversity of communal intestinal bacteria have been associated with a wide array of disorders such as multiple sclerosis, autism, depression and schizophrenia. There are, of course, many other contributors to these complex illnesses and oxidative stress will most certainly play a role as well. SIBO is diagnosed using a breath test and is often confused with IBS. SIBO is the result of an overgrowth and imbalance of bacteria in the small intestine that should not be in that part of the gut. Surgery, a poor diet, or infection can cause SIBO. Ageing, stress and adrenal imbalance can increase the risk for SIBO as the Migrating Motor Complex (MMC) becomes less functional. The MMC is responsible for sweeping bacteria through the small intestine so that it doesn't back up. Another key link to gut motility and constipation/diarrhea issues is that serotonin also affects peristalsis (stomach contractions that move food through the gut). A lack of serotonin production not only results in depression but causes gut issues.

Genes that can fight or fuel inflammation
Variations in certain genes such as FADS (fatty acid desaturase) have been associated with a greater risk of inflammation when there is an imbalance in the omega-6:omega-3 ratio. If you are sensitive to these fats, this imbalance creates an inflammatory pathway and can contribute to chronic diseases. This is especially true when it comes to processed vegetable oils used for

fast foods and other convenience foods. Even a 'healthy' salad from the deli counter may have too much sunflower oil, and the seemingly healthy salad is actually adding to the individual's inflammatory load.

Our ancient ancestors ate a diet that was much higher in omega-3 fats compared to omega-6 fats. This gradual decline in the ratio of omega-3:omega-6 fats may have contributed to the rise in chronic inflammatory disorders that have become so common. Processed fats and carbohydrates in fast foods have become a scourge and this imbalance is one of many that have contributed to the obesity pandemic.

Chronic inflammation is being commonly recognized as a significant contributor to heart disease. An anti-inflammatory diet that is high in omega-3 (flaxseeds, oily fish) and exercise are highly recommended to reduce this risk.

Genetic variations in inflammatory genes may result in a higher predisposition to inflammatory conditions such as rheumatoid arthritis or insulin resistance. For those individuals, and for almost everyone else, it would be best to steer clear of refined carbohydrates, highly processed confectionary, and processed oils. Following a diet rich in anti-inflammatory nutrients such as ginger, curcumin, resveratrol and omega-3 oils can help calm the storm.

Anti-inflammatory ingredients for preventative action

Did you know that chocolate can be good for you?
Don't get too excited! Obviously, a diet high in processed sugars, fats and artificial ingredients cannot be remedied with a bar of milky chocolate. It's the powerful polyphenols in the cocoa powder that we are looking for. The polyphenols found in cocoa and dark chocolate have anti-inflammatory functions and can switch on important signalling pathways that stimulate changes in gene expression and the immune response. Cocoa polyphenols also protect our cardiovascular system by activating the gene eNOS (nitric oxide synthase). This results in the release of nitric oxide, which helps increase vasodilation, and thus protects our arteries from atherosclerosis (hardening of the arteries). This anti-inflammatory action is not only

confined to the arteries in our hearts, but also most importantly the neurovascular system of our brains. Cocoa can protect the nerves from injury and inflammation and protect the skin from oxidative damage from the sun's UV rays, and researchers have found that regular consumption of cocoa mixed with skimmed milk improved cholesterol levels in some people.

The colour purple
Proanthocyanins (once you get over the pronunciation) and anthocyanins are marvellous antioxidants that give fruit and vegetables their red, blue or purple colour.

There is no quick fix or miracle cure, and a daily handful of cranberries and strawberries are not the answer to all our questions. Digestion is not a simple plumbing system that starts in the mouth and ends up precisely in our vital organs. There are many barriers to the bioavailability of these brilliant molecules once they reach the complex and very individual human gut. However, by changing our diet to include a 'rainbow' of plant foods, we can achieve a greater level of health by decreasing or avoiding chronic inflammation.

Cold-pressed virgin olive oil
The mainstay of the Mediterranean diet, olive oil, has proved to be highly effective as an anti-inflammatory agent. It is found in fish, seeds and nuts.

Virgin olive oil is a functional food, which means it is a biologically active food that can impact gene expression. Besides its high concentration of healthy monounsaturated fatty acids (MUFAs), virgin olive oil contains a high percentage of polyphenols. Polyphenols are a member of the family of phytochemicals. Anti-inflammatory polyphenols are also found in curcumin (in turmeric), red wine, tea, quercetin (in apples and onions) and dark chocolate.

Studies have shown that the polyphenol oleic acid in virgin olive oil can modify gene expression in processes involved in oxidative stress and inflammation. Researchers have found that virgin olive oil is highly beneficial for reducing oxidative stress which results in multiple disorders such as cardiovascular disease and type 2 diabetes.

Omega-3 fatty acids found in fish, seeds and nuts
In 1929, the biochemists Evans and Burr discovered essential fatty acids. They showed that humans do not possess the necessary enzymes for breaking down the double bonds found in omega-3 and omega-6 fatty acids and that they would have to be obtained through diet.

Cardiovascular disease (CVD) is the leading cause of death for men and women and includes disorders of the heart as well as blood vessels. The World Health Organization reports that four out of five CVD deaths are due to heart attack and stroke. CVD within blood vessels in the brain is known as cerebrovascular disease. This can be seen in certain types of dementia and Alzheimer's disease.

Inflammation plays a central role in the development of CVD and autoimmune disorders. Growing evidence demonstrates the anti-inflammatory effects of omega-3 fatty acids in reducing circulating levels of inflammatory cytokines. The benefits of omega-3 fatty acids in our diet demonstrate a wide range of actions that are beneficial for the cardiovascular system.

Plant omega-3 and animal omega-3 fatty acids
Our ancient ancestors consumed a higher percentage of omega-3 fatty acids than omega-6 fats. Up until World War II, those ratios remained relatively high. Due mostly to changes in food production, industrialization and lifestyles that are centered around 'fast' food and less hunter-gathering, the modern diet is now disproportionately higher in omega-6 fats than omega-3 fats, the ratio has altered dramatically. Higher risk individuals should try to consume more omega-3s than omega-6s and generally reduce their intake of processed foods.

Some examples of omega-6 fats are corn oil, sunflower oil, mayonnaise, commercial salad dressing, cottonseed oil and sesame seed oil.

Plants such as walnuts, flaxseeds, chia seeds, spirulina, chlorella, seaweed, hemp seeds, edamame, kidney beans, soybeans and echium seed oil are good sources of omega-3.

Fish, particularly oily fish, contain high levels of omega-3 fatty acids. Good sources are salmon, mackerel, sardines and herring.

Your Healing Kitchen

Anti-inflammatory foods include: oily fish, salmon, herring, mackerel, sardines, flaxseeds, avocado, nuts, seeds, ginger, green and black tea, apples, onions, capers, peanuts, blueberries, blackberries, prunes, red cabbage, aubergine/eggplant, rhubarb, beetroot/beet, red wine, raspberries, cherries, cranberries, strawberries, slow-cooked tomatoes, red peppers/red bell peppers, carrots, asparagus, papaya, watermelon, guava, asparagus, egg yolks, oranges, apricots, sweet potato, kale, spinach.

Fast food

- Glass of unsweetened pomegranate juice – *great for high blood pressure*
- Cup (or vat!) of green tea
- Bone broth soup
- Bowl of frozen red grapes
- Spinach and chicken (organic) salad
- Handful of Brazil nuts, cashew nuts and dried cranberries *(also great for oxidative stress)*
- Fruit salad with raspberries, strawberries and cherries
- Chopped pineapple and kiwi (skin on) – *bromelain, a protein-digesting enzyme in pineapples, increases the absorption of quercetin*
- 85% dark chocolate

Easy recipes

BREAKFAST
Baked cinnamon apples
Melon, ginger and chia seed fruit salad

MAIN MEALS
Butternut squash, pear and leek soup
Pan-fried mackerel and capers
with rhubarb-and-ginger salsa
Baked salmon with caper salsa verde
Southern polenta-and-flaxseed chicken wings
Baked Parmesan courgette fries
Soba noodle, tofu and vegetable salad with miso dressing

SNACKS AND TREATS
Guacamole with red pepper 'scoopers'
Flourless dark chocolate cake with red berry coulis
Turmeric and ginger cookies

DRINKS
Strawberry and basil lemonade
Pomegranate slushy

Breakfast

Baked cinnamon apples

Serves 2

An apple a day keeps the doctor away… Apples are high in fibre, vitamins C and E, potassium and magnesium.

Don't peel your apples, because the quercetin is found mostly in the skin. Quercetin has antioxidant and anti-inflammatory properties and also has benefits for exercise performance and reducing blood pressure. It is found in onions, apples, capers, dark cherries, blueberries, blackberries, dark chocolate and olive oil.

Apples have been shown to have an anti-inflammatory effect based on their polyphenol content.

Pectin found in apples is almost completely fermented in the gut and contributes to a healthy human gut flora. Pectin has a major role in lowering cholesterol.

- 2 Bramley (cooking) apples
- 2 dates
- 30 g/1 oz raisins
- juice of 2 oranges
- 1 tbsp clear honey
- 3 star anise
- ½ tbsp cinnamon
- finely grated zest of 1 orange

1. Preheat the oven to 200°C/180°C fan/gas mark 6. Core the apples and place them in an ovenproof baking dish. Push a date into each apple's empty core and fill the rest of the hole with raisins – sprinkle any remaining raisins around the dish.
2. Pour the orange juice and honey into the tray and add the star anise, then sprinkle the cinnamon and orange zest over the apples
3. Bake for 40–45 minutes, until the apples burst and go crispy on the outside.

Melon, ginger and chia seed fruit salad

Serves 2

Melons are high in carotenoids, which are anti-inflammatory and protective against age-related eye disease.

- 1 ripe melon
- 3 cms of ginger root, peeled and grated
- drizzle of honey
- 1 tsp chia seeds
- handful of red grapes, halved

1. Cut the melon into slices, arrange on a plate and sprinkle with the ginger. Drizzle with a little honey and scatter with chia seeds and red grapes. Fresh, easy delicious!

Tip: Buying melons can be tricky, but a general rule of thumb is that if they smell sweet, they will be good! I like to use Ogen and cantaloupe melons.

Main meals

Butternut squash, pear and leek soup

Serves 4

The list of butternut squash's health benefits is long. It contains vitamins C and A, potassium, magnesium and many anti-inflammatory carotenoids. Butternut squash retains its vitamin C even after cooking.

- 2 tbsp butter
- 1 large leek, trimmed and sliced
- 750 g/1 lb 10 oz butternut squash, peeled and chopped into 1 cm/½ in cubes
- 2 ripe pears, cored and chopped
- 1 l/35 fl oz/4⅓ cups chicken stock (use an organic stock cube if possible)
- salt and freshly ground black pepper

To serve (optional)
- 1 small red chilli, deseeded and finely chopped
- feta, crumbled
- pumpkin seeds

1. Melt the butter in a large, lidded saucepan until foaming. Add the leek, butternut squash and pears and cook with the lid on for about 10 minutes on a low heat, until everything is buttery and soft.
2. Add the stock, bring to the boil and simmer for a further 20 minutes with the lid off.
3. When the butternut squash has softened, liquidize the soup and season with salt and pepper, to taste.
4. Top with the chilli, crumbled feta or pumpkin seeds (if using).

Pan-fried mackerel and capers with rhubarb-and-ginger salsa

Serves 2

This is a great all-round anti-inflammatory recipe, which you can also use for oxidative stress. High in fibre, calcium, vitamins K and C, iron and magnesium, rhubarb is a wonderful seasonal go-to ingredient.

Salsa
- 125 g/4½ oz rhubarb, cut into 1 cm/½ in pieces
- 1 red chilli, deseeded and finely chopped
- small knob of fresh ginger, peeled and grated
- 2 tbsp clear honey
- 1 small onion, peeled and finely diced (optional)
- 2 fresh mackerel fillets
- glug of olive oil
- 1 tbsp chopped capers
- 2 tsp sherry vinegar

1. First, make the salsa. Put the rhubarb and 100 ml/3½ fl oz/7 tbsp water in a small saucepan and bring to the boil. Simmer for 5 minutes, then strain off the water and allow the rhubarb to cool. Add the chilli, ginger, honey and onion (if using). Season with salt and taste, adding more honey if needed.
2. To prepare the fish, heat the oil in a frying pan and, when hot, carefully place the mackerel in the pan, skin side down. Fry for 2 minutes on a high heat, then, using a palate knife, carefully flip the fish over and cook for a further 2 minutes. Add the capers and vinegar to the pan and cook for a further 30 seconds.
3. Remove the mackerel and capers from the pan and serve immediately with the rhubarb salsa.

Baked salmon with caper salsa verde

Serves 4

Capers are high in quercetin, an antioxidant to support oxidative stress and inflammation.

Omega-3 fatty acids found in salmon are anti-inflammatory and anti-ageing. Salmon is also high in astaxanthin, which protects against a wide range of diseases and is protective against oxidative stress. Omega-3s are particularly beneficial for skin health.

- 4 wild-caught salmon fillets
- coconut oil, for greasing
- juice of ½ lemon
- freshly ground black pepper

Salsa
- handful of dill, stalks removed
- handful of mint, stalks removed
- handful of parsley, stalks removed
- handful of chives
- 1½ tbsp wholegrain mustard
- 2 tbsp capers
- 2 tbsp pine nuts
- 100 g/3½ oz pitted green olives
- juice of 1½ lemons
- 3 anchovies (from a jar or tin)
- 1 tbsp maple syrup

1. Preheat the oven to 200°C/180°C fan/gas mark 6.
2. Put the salmon on a lightly oiled baking sheet. Squeeze over ¼ of the lemon juice and season with pepper. Bake in the oven for 12–14 minutes, or until cooked through.
3. To make the salsa verde, put the herbs, mustard, capers, pine nuts, olives and anchovies and lemon juice into a food processor and pulse until roughly chopped. Add the maple syrup to taste – you want the salsa to be tart, so go easy with the sweetness.
4. Pile the salsa verde on top of the salmon fillets and serve with rice or a green salad.

Southern polenta-and-flaxseed chicken wings

Serves 4

Lutein found in polenta (yellow corn) is protective against age-related macular degeneration and is also beneficial for cardiovascular health. Flaxseeds are high in magnesium and omega-3. This recipe is also good for methylation.

- 1 large egg
- 175 ml/5½ fl oz/⅔ cup buttermilk
- 1 kg/2 lb 4 oz organic chicken wings (tips removed)
- 115 g/4 oz polenta
- 2 tbsp ground flaxseeds
- 100 g/3½ oz wholemeal/wholewheat flour (or gluten-free flour)
- pinch of sea salt
- olive oil, for greasing and drizzling

1. Beat the egg and buttermilk together in a large bowl until evenly combined, then add the chicken wings. Cover and leave in the fridge for up to 24 hours (3 hours minimum).
2. When you are ready to cook the chicken, preheat the oven to 220°C/200°C fan/gas mark 7.
3. Combine the polenta with the flaxseeds, flour and salt in a large, shallow dish. Shake the buttermilk marinade off the chicken wings and dip each wing in the polenta mix to coat.
4. Lay the coated chicken on a greased (or silicone) baking tray. Drizzle a little olive oil over the top of them, so they don't stick. Roast for 1 hour, turning halfway through the cooking time.

Baked Parmesan courgette fries

Serves 4

Courgettes/zucchini are high in beta-carotene and lutein and zeaxanthin. These anti-inflammatory molecules play a role in eye health and overall cellular protection.

- 55 g/2 oz fine polenta
- 3 tbsp grated Parmesan cheese
- 2 eggs, beaten
- 4 courgettes/zucchini, cut into batons

1. Preheat the oven to 220°C/200°C fan/gas mark 7.
2. Stir the polenta and Parmesan cheese together in a shallow bowl. Whisk the eggs in a separate shallow bowl. Working in batches, dip the courgette batons into the egg, shake to remove any excess, and roll in the cheesy polenta mixture to coat. Transfer the coated courgette batons to a silicone baking sheet in a single layer. Bake in the preheated oven, turning once, for 20–25 minutes until golden and crisp.

Soba noodle, tofu and vegetable salad with miso dressing

Serves 2

Red peppers/red bell peppers and spinach contain lutein, an anti-inflammatory ingredient which is protective against age-related macular degeneration.

- 270 g/9½ oz dried soba noodles
- 100 g/3½ oz sugar snap peas
- 1 large carrot, peeled, cut into matchsticks
- 2 tbsp olive oil
- 200 g/7 oz firm tofu
- 4 small radishes, thinly sliced
- 1 red pepper/red bell pepper, finely chopped
- 100 g/3½ oz baby spinach leaves
- handful of sunflower seeds

Dressing
- 2 tbsp rice wine vinegar
- 1 tbsp miso paste
- 1½ tbsp olive oil
- 2 tsp soy sauce or tamari (wheat-free soy sauce)
- 1 tsp finely grated fresh ginger
- 1 tsp Dijon mustard
- 1 tsp maple syrup

1. Cook the noodles in a large saucepan of lightly salted boiling water until *al dente*, adding the sugar snap peas and carrot during the last 30 seconds of cooking. Drain and set aside.
2. Pour a splash of olive oil into a frying pan and cook the tofu block for 2 minutes on each side, or until light golden in colour. Cut the tofu into 1 cm/½ in strips.
3. Add the tofu, radishes, red pepper, spinach and sunflower seeds to the noodles and other vegetables. Toss to combine.
4. Put the dressing ingredients in a jar with a lid and shake to combine. Pour the dressing over the noodle mixture and serve.

Snacks and treats

Guacamole

Serves 4

Quercetin, found in onions, is anti-inflammatory. Tomatoes are high in lycopene, a carotenoid that has anti-inflammatory properties and is protective against heart disease and stroke. The benefits are increased when combined with olive oil.

- 2 large, ripe avocados, cut into small pieces
- ½ onion, peeled and very finely chopped
- juice of 1 lime
- 1 garlic clove, crushed
- 1 tomato, finely chopped
- 1 tbsp olive oil
- pinch of salt and pepper
- 1 red chilli, deseeded and finely chopped (optional)
- 1 red pepper/red bell pepper, cut into strips, to serve

1. To make the guacamole, mix all the ingredients, except the red pepper, in a small bowl and taste – it may need more lime juice, salt or garlic, depending on how you like it!
2. Serve the guacamole with the red pepper strips (use them to scoop up the dip).

Flourless dark chocolate cake with red berry coulis

Serves 8

Cacao is a fantastic nutrigenomic ingredient. It contains more phenolic antioxidants than most foods. It is also great also for oxidative stress and methylation. Cocoa is the roasted powder derived from ground cacao beans. Raw cacao is made by cold-pressing un-roasted cacao beans.

- rapeseed oil for greasing
- 250 g/9 oz dark chocolate, broken into pieces
- 250 g/9 oz butter
- 1 tbsp strong coffee
- 8 eggs, separated
- 100 g/3½ oz soft light brown sugar
- 160 g/5½ oz golden caster sugar
- 85 g/3 oz cocoa powder
- ½ tsp salt

1. Grease a 23 cm/9 in cake tin/cake pan and line with greaseproof paper.
2. Melt the chocolate and butter together in a heatproof bowl set over, but not touching, a pan of simmering water. Stir until smooth, then stir in the coffee and set aside to cool slightly.
3. Preheat the oven to 180°C/160°C fan/gas mark 4.
4. Beat the egg yolks and sugar together and whisk until doubled in volume. Sift the cocoa powder on top of the egg mixture (don't just dump it in or you'll get lumps). Add the salt, then mix (on a low speed if using a blender) until the cocoa is well combined.
5. Put the egg whites in another large bowl and whisk to the soft-peak stage.
6. Gently fold the melted chocolate mixture into the egg-yolk mixture. Fold ⅓ of the egg white into the mixture to loosen it before very carefully folding the rest in, until the mixture is no longer streaky but an even, rich brown.
7. Spoon the mixture into the cake tin and cook in the oven for 40–50 minutes until just set on top, then allow to cool in the tin on a wire rack.

Red berry coulis

Serves 8

Red berries contain high levels of proanthocyanins, which are recommended for inflammation and oxidative stress.

- 300 g/10½ oz frozen red berries
- 1 tbsp caster sugar (optional)

1. Thaw the berries for 2 minutes in a microwave. Place in a blender, and blend until smooth. Press the coulis through a sieve/strainer using a wooden spoon. Stir in the sugar if using.

Turmeric and ginger cookies

Makes approximately 9 cookies

Turmeric is beneficial for inflammatory bowel disease (IBD) and IBS sufferers and ginger helps to relieve nausea. Ginger is a powerful antioxidant and anti-inflammatory.

- 70 g/2½ oz coconut oil
- 50 ml/3 tbsp maple syrup
- 65 g/2¼ oz ground almonds
- 65 g/2¼ oz mixed seeds
- 125 g/4½ oz gluten-free oats
- 20 g/½ oz knob of grated ginger root, peeled
- 1 tsp cinnamon
- 1 tsp ground ginger
- 1 tsp freshly grated turmeric or 1 tsp ground turmeric
- 1 tsp baking powder
- 1 ripe banana, mashed

1. Preheat the oven to 200°C/180°C fan/gas mark 6.
2. In a large saucepan heat the coconut oil and stir in the maple syrup. Add the other ingredients and, using a wooden spoon, stir well to incorporate everything.
3. Put rounded tablespoons of the mixture onto a non-stick baking sheet and bake for 15 minutes, or until light golden in colour. Allow to cool before lifting off the tray.

Drinks

Strawberry and basil lemonade

Serves 1

Strawberries and basil contain antioxidants, and basil provides calcium and vitamin K.

- 1 small punnet of strawberries
- sprig of fresh basil
- juice of 2 lemons
- handful of ice cubes
- 2 tbsp maple syrup
- sprig of fresh mint, to decorate

1. Put the strawberries, basil, lemon juice, ice and maple syrup in a jug with 120 ml/4 fl oz/½ cup water and blend with a handheld blender. Serve in a chilled glass with the mint on top.

Pomegranate slushy

Serves 1

Pomegranates are very high in antioxidants. They are anti-inflammatory, effective in reducing high blood pressure and have numerous benefits for heart health.

- 100 ml/3½ fl oz/7 tbsp unsweetened pomegranate juice
- 100 ml/3½ fl oz/7 tbsp apple juice
- handful of ice cubes
- fresh pomegranate seeds, to decorate

1. Blitz the pomegranate and apple juice with the ice in a blender and serve in a glass with the pomegranate seeds scattered on top.

Chapter 3

Oxidative Stress

We all know how essential oxygen is to life on earth and that without oxygen our lives would end quite abruptly.

When cells use oxygen to produce energy, this everyday process creates something called free radicals. These free radicals are very necessary for normal cellular function but can also turn nasty when the balance is disturbed.

Free radicals are produced when oxygen splits into single atoms. These highly reactive atoms have one or more unpaired electrons. Electrons like to be in pairs, so these free radicals scavenge the body seeking out other electrons to pair with. This causes damage to cells, proteins and DNA.

Oxidative stress is necessary in small amounts
Free radicals play a dual role as both toxic and beneficial compounds – they can either be helpful or harmful to the human body. In a moderate dose, they are useful and perform a great job at fighting off invading bacteria and other microbes and are vital to enhancing the immune system.

When this delicate balance is disrupted and there is an over-production of free radicals, oxidative damage to cells occurs and contributes to human diseases such as cancer, neurological disorders, cardiovascular disease, diabetes and pulmonary disease. High levels of oxidative stress can also contribute to accelerated aging of the skin and can be seen in the form of wrinkles and prematurely aged skin.

What does oxidative stress look like?

Picture an apple that is cut in half and turns brown in a short time, or a piece of metal that has gone through the same process of oxidation and has become rusty.

Oxidative stress in a human body, as opposed to an apple core, is the result of a constant overload of free radicals that are not effectively neutralized or destroyed by antioxidants.

Fried foods, sugar and processed foods don't do us any good at all. Cigarette smoke, pollution, chemicals in our water, and pesticides in our food place continual stress on our cells and this needs to be counteracted by antioxidants and detoxifying enzymes that are made in our bodies, but also need to be eaten regularly in the form of fruit, vegetables and tree nuts.

Besides these external influences of processed foods and pollution, our genes play a large part in our risk for disease or our potential for great health. Our built-in antioxidant kit is largely determined by how effective our genes are at producing the correct amounts of enzymes necessary to keep things in check.

Oxidative stress genes – our protection and defence system

Our body manufactures enzymes to neutralize and mop up the free radicals that damage DNA, fats and protein cells. It's important to know that no organs or systems in our bodies operate on their own. It's all about teamwork and it all begins with digestion. Before the nutrients have even entered our bloodstream, digestive enzymes are released from the moment we set eyes on the meal before us. Our moods determine a lot as well. If we eat on the run or in a stressed state, we are unconsciously releasing way more stress hormones (glucocorticoids) than digestives enzymes.

Once the nutrients are broken down into smaller components during digestion and then absorption, the magic or mishaps really begin. As always, it depends on our genes as to how effective or defective our bodies will be at absorbing and transporting our 'food', which has now been broken down and converted into compounds of amino acids, glucose molecules, and fatty acids.

The gateway to health lies in our ability to neutralize and protect our cells from free radical damage and we have an awesome security team at work.

The terminology gets complex, but don't be put off! Enzymes have many, often unpronounceable names and they have been shortened by scientists. A simple way of knowing if we're referring to an enzyme is to know that enzymes all end in 'ase'. SOD2 is called superoxide dismutase 2. GPx1 is glutathione peroxidase 1 and CAT is catalase.

The team leader and first line of defence in the system is this SOD2. For SOD2 to effectively do its job of protecting our cells against illness and attack, it relies on helpers or cofactors to complete the team. These guys are minerals that most of us have heard about but not thought too deeply about either. Without enough manganese, magnesium or zinc, SOD2 cannot get the job done effectively.

To optimise your defence system and protect your cells from oxidative damage and chronic disease, you need to be supplying the essential nutrients. Pumpkin seeds, flaxseeds, sesame seeds and nuts are not just for squirrels and budgies. They are a great source of minerals and cofactors that work in a similar way to spark plugs in a car. Without the necessary 'spark plugs' the antioxidant enzymes cannot perform their job effectively.

GPx1 is a vital team member. This enzyme is essential for recycling the critical antioxidant glutathione. Glutathione is needed to protect our cells from oxidative damage from free radicals. For GPx1 to operate effectively, it needs selenium. Top of the list for this are Brazil nuts, but mushrooms, turkey and sardines contain selenium too. Glutathione is a sulfur molecule, so think back to those foods high in sulfur such as eggs, broccoli, cauliflower, garlic, onions, and leeks.

The enzyme catalase (CAT), plays a protective role against cancer, diabetes and neurodegenerative diseases and requires the cofactors (helper molecules), manganese as well as iron to function optimally. Good sources of manganese are pineapples, brown rice, sweet potatoes, spinach, pumpkin seeds, oats, nuts, beans, clams, mussels, and oysters. Make sure you check your iron/ferritin levels regularly. Too much and too little are both harmful to health.

Cofactors are needed to enhance gene expression. To get the best out of our antioxidant system, we need to make sure we have adequate cofactors in our diet. Selenium, zinc, magnesium, manganese and iron are all necessary in the correct amounts.

The far-reaching effects of oxidative stress
Emotional stress and depressed mood are associated with a huge release of free radicals. An added stressor in these circumstances is so-called 'comfort' foods such as ice-cream, crisps, candy bars and fast-food burgers. Sadly, these do not bring comfort to our antioxidant system and being overweight increases oxidative stress signals.

Insulin resistance is an inflammatory condition that may result in oxidative damage to sensitive cells. There is a self-perpetuating cycle between oxidative stress and inflammation that not only results in inflammatory weight gain but also has far-reaching effects on our emotional health, brain function and most of our other essential organs.

Insulin is a hormone made in the beta cells of the pancreas. After eating, the pancreas releases insulin into the blood so that it can help glucose (blood sugar) enter cells in your muscles, body fat or liver, where it is used for energy. In people with insulin resistance, the muscles and liver do not respond well to insulin, so the body keeps producing more insulin in order to keep blood glucose within a normal range. Continuous glucose 'spiking' has been shown to increase oxidative stress because the beta cells in the pancreas that produce insulin are not well protected by the antioxidant enzymes.

The nervous system and the brain are particularly sensitive to oxidative stress. One reason for this is that the brain has a large demand for oxygen, which leads to free radical release. The cell walls of the brain are high in polyunsaturated fatty acids which forms part of the highly sensitive blood–brain barrier. The blood–brain barrier is the protective layer that keeps harmful pathogens out but still has to allow vital nutrients to pass into the brain. Protecting the integrity of this vital barrier is essential for cognitive function. A diet high in omega-3 fats and phosphatidylserine is always a brainy idea. Good sources of phosphatidylserine include soy, egg yolks and liver. Low levels of antioxidant enzymes in the brain make it vulnerable to free radicals.

Brief episodes of anxiety caused by public speaking or even the physical stress of a hard exercise session are normal responses to immediate stress and anxiety. However, when anxiety or intense exercise become constant and excessive, this can result in physical or psychological disorders. Depression is known to be accompanied by inflammation and oxidative stress, often with low levels of antioxidants such as vitamin E, zinc and coenzyme Q10.

Although each neurological disorder will have its own particular structure, disorders of the nervous system are mostly underpinned by oxidative stress and inflammation.

Sulfur is an important element in all biological systems, but particularly important in the antioxidant system because sulfur-containing compounds can efficiently form a protective line of defence against free radicals. Unfortunately, exposure to mercury, arsenic, lead, and pesticides can overwhelm the sulfur-containing antioxidant system and drive the body into a heightened oxidative stress cycle. There are concerns that some populations are not eating enough sulfur-containing foods that offer protection to our bodies and vulnerable brains.

The important sulfur amino acids are found in whole eggs, meat, chicken, fish and dairy. For vegans, Brazil nuts, quinoa, spinach, broccoli, cauliflower, garlic, onions, sesame seeds, chickpeas, beans and oats are viable sources.

Chronic and degenerative disorders of our bodies and brains such as cancer, IBD, IBS, arthritis, autoimmune disorders, premature ageing, cardiovascular disease and neurodegenerative disorders (Parkinson's disease, Alzheimer's disease) have all been associated in some respect with oxidative stress, inflammation and detoxification processes.

Preventative nutrition and personal health management begin way upstream

Balance is key to maintaining the sensitive antioxidant defence systems, and keeping chronic inflammation at bay. Signals and triggers begin way upstream in the cells and the chemical messages are passed along the route, influencing metabolism in multiple ways. Once again, the Nrf2 pathway can be upregulated and used as the master switch to optimise health outcomes. By making sure you are eating your broccoli or fermented vegetables, you can be activating thousands of protective genes in your body and helping to arm your internal defences while protecting your DNA from damage.

While this territory and terminology may be unfamiliar to you, the impact of eating foods that can have a widespread and positive result on your health is the focus of many studies and research.

Eating a variety of foods is not just essential to life; it also promotes good health and helps to prevent disease. Oxidative damage that is left unrepaired can lead to certain cancers. Evidence suggests that the risk of cancer for most cancer sites was twice as high in individuals whose intake of fruit and vegetables was low, compared with those whose intake was high.

A study of people in Finland, where there is a high intake of apples and onions (containing quercetin), showed a reduced risk of death from heart disease. In Hawaii, consumption of apples and onions was found to reduce the risk of lung cancer. Apples with their skin on, and onions, are two simple foods to include in our daily diets.

Your Healing Kitchen

Ingredients known to support oxidative stress include: beetroot/beet, pomegranate juice, cocoa powder, bananas, peas, cashew nuts, walnuts, almonds, pumpkin seeds, quinoa, brown rice, lentils, barley, millet, cocoa, dark leafy greens, mushrooms, cabbage, squash, oysters, shrimp, prawns and dark chocolate.

Fast food

It's always great to have a fallback plan when you're dashing around but want to remain healthy and snack on things that are good rather than bad for you. Here are a few ideas that will help you stay on track if you're on the go or need to buy convenience food:

- Bag of mixed seeds (pumpkin, sunflower and sesame)
- Prawn cocktail
- Prawn and spinach salad
- Handful of Brazil nuts
- Supermarket quinoa salad
- Vegetable curry + brown rice
- 4 squares of 85+% dark chocolate

Easy recipes

BREAKFAST
Super-speedy-no-kneady-seedy bread
Garlic mushrooms

MAIN MEALS
Pearl barley and porcini mushroom broth
Chicken, spinach and lentil saag
Allspice red cabbage braised with apples
and maple syrup
Caponata (Italian ratatouille)
Roasted cauliflower, pomegranate
and quinoa salad in a jar
Spicy Sichuan ginger prawns
Chicken satay with spicy peanut dipping sauce
Asparagus roasted with garlic and sesame seeds
Black bean chocolate chilli
Spicy mango guacamole
Beetroot tzatziki
Brazil nut and tarragon pesto
Mexican quinoa salad with orange and lime dressing

DRINKS
Chocolate, banana and peanut milkshake
Cashew nut and cinnamon milk

Breakfast

Super-speedy-no-kneady-seedy bread

Makes 1 loaf

- 500 g/1 lb 2 oz spelt flour (avoid if gluten intolerant)
- 150 g/5½ oz mixed seeds
- 2 small packets quick yeast (14 g/½ oz or 4 tsp)
- ½ tsp salt
- 500 ml/17 fl oz/2 cups + 2 tbsp warm water

1. Preheat the oven to 200°C/180°C fan/gas mark 6. Line a 25 cm loaf tin with greaseproof paper.
2. Mix all the ingredients together in a bowl, then transfer the dough into the loaf tin and bake for 1 hour.
3. NB: The bread will rise, but is quite dense in texture.
4. Serve with Garlic mushrooms (see below).

Tip: Slice the whole loaf as soon as it is cool enough to handle. Then put a small sheet of greaseproof paper between each slice and freeze. I toast a slice straight from the freezer, which gives me just enough time to make the Garlic mushrooms.

Garlic mushrooms

Serves 1

Mushrooms contain selenium, a powerful antioxidant and a 'helper molecule' in the oxidative stress pathway. Mushrooms provide numerous health benefits due to their medicinal properties. Beta-glucans found in mushrooms can support the immune system and provide prebiotics, vital for gut health.

- 2 tbsp olive oil
- 1 garlic clove, crushed
- 1 generous handful of button mushrooms, thinly sliced
- pinch of salt

1. Heat the oil in a frying pan, then gently fry the garlic for 1 minute. Add the mushrooms and cook for a further 3 minutes.
2. Season with salt and serve the mushrooms and their juices on a slice of toasted seedy bread.

Main meals

Pearl barley and porcini mushroom broth

Serves 2

Pearl barley is a source of protein and is very high in fibre. It is also a good source of magnesium, potassium and calcium. Manganese and copper are also found in barley – who knew barley was so good for us?! Note, however, that barley is not gluten-free.

- handful of dried porcini mushrooms
- 2 tbsp olive oil
- 1 small onion, peeled and finely chopped
- 1 celery stick, chopped
- 2 carrots, peeled and diced
- 225 g/8 oz assorted mushrooms, sliced
- 1.2 l/40 fl oz/5 cups vegetable or chicken stock
- 90 g/3¼ oz pearl barley
- salt and freshly ground black pepper

1. Put the porcini mushrooms in a heatproof bowl and cover with boiling water. Soak for 10 minutes, then drain and chop them.
2. Heat the oil in a deep saucepan, then add the onion, celery, carrots and assorted mushrooms. Fry gently for 5 minutes or until soft.
3. Add the porcini mushrooms, stock and pearl barley and simmer gently for 25 minutes. Season with salt and pepper, to taste.

Chicken, spinach and lentil saag

Serves 4

This recipe is also great for inflammation and methylation.

- 1 red chilli, deseeded
- 2 garlic cloves, peeled
- 3 cm piece of ginger root, peeled
- 1 onion, peeled and roughly chopped
- 1 tsp olive oil
- 1 tsp ground cumin
- 1 tsp ground coriander/cilantro
- 1 tsp garam masala
- ½ tsp freshly grated or ground turmeric
- 4 skinless chicken thighs, cut into strips
- 150 g/5½ oz red split lentils
- 1 x 400 g/14 oz tin chopped tomatoes
- salt and freshly ground black pepper
- juice of 1 lime
- 1 tsp dark maple syrup
- ½ bag baby spinach leaves

1. Put the chilli, garlic, ginger and onion in a small blender and blitz to a paste.
2. Heat the oil in a large pan and fry the paste for a couple minutes until fragrant. Add the spices and cook for another minute.
3. Add the chicken and coat in the spices. Cook for 5 minutes, then add the lentils and tomatoes along with 1½ tins of water and simmer for 25 minutes.
4. Season with salt and pepper, to taste, then add the lime juice, maple syrup and spinach and stir until the spinach has wilted.

Allspice red cabbage braised with apples and maple syrup

Serves 4

Red cabbage is high in anthocyanins, a potent antioxidant and anti-inflammatory. Apples are high in flavonols (which may, among other benefits, play a special role in protecting the brain) and antioxidants when cooked. Dark maple syrup contains antioxidants.

- 25 g/1 oz butter
- 1 large onion, peeled and finely sliced
- ½ tsp ground allspice
- ¼ tsp freshly grated nutmeg
- 1 small red cabbage, core and tough outer leaves discarded, finely sliced
- 1 Bramley apple, peeled, cored and grated
- 4 tbsp red wine vinegar
- 2 tbsp dark maple syrup
- salt and freshly ground black pepper
- 2 tbsp redcurrant jelly

1. Melt the butter in a saucepan with a tight-fitting lid over a medium heat. Cook the onion, uncovered, for 5 minutes until soft but not browned.
2. Stir in the spices, then add the cabbage, apple, vinegar and maple syrup plus 100 ml/3½ fl oz/7 tbsp cold water. Keep stirring until the ingredients are combined and season generously with salt and pepper.
3. Bring to the boil, then cover tightly and simmer for about 1 hour, stirring occasionally, until the cabbage is very tender and the liquid has evaporated. Stir in the redcurrant jelly.
4. This dish is great served with turkey or a roasted sweet potato.

Caponata (Italian ratatouille)

Serves 4

Aubergines/eggplants and tomatoes contain high amounts of anthocyanin and antioxidants to combat oxidative stress and inflammation. (Avoid tomatoes and aubergines if you are sensitive to lectins.)

- 4 tbsp olive oil
- 3 aubergines/eggplants, chopped into small cubes
- 1 onion, peeled and finely chopped
- ½ celery stick, finely diced
- 1 x 390 g carton chopped tomatoes
- 50 g/1¾ oz pitted green olives
- 30 ml/1 fl oz/2 tbsp red wine vinegar
- 1½ tbsp maple syrup
- salt and freshly ground black pepper
- 3 tbsp capers
- handful chopped parsley leaves

1. Heat 2 tablespoons of the olive oil in a saucepan and brown the aubergines on a medium heat for 10 minutes. When cooked, set them aside to cool.
2. In a separate saucepan, heat the remaining olive oil and sauté the onion and the celery for 5 minutes, then add the tomatoes, olives, vinegar and maple syrup. Bring to the boil and simmer for 15 minutes. Season with salt and pepper.
3. Add the cooled aubergine and the capers. Transfer to a large bowl, add the parsley and mix well. This dish can be served hot or cold.

Roasted cauliflower, pomegranate and quinoa salad in a jar

Serves 2

This recipe is ideal for anyone wanting to reduce their gluten intake. Pomegranates are beneficial for countering oxidative stress. This recipe is also great for detoxification and methylation.

Salads in jars keep nice and fresh, and when layered not only taste great but look awesome too!

- 1 small cauliflower, cut into florets
- 3 tbsp olive oil
- 1 tsp ground cumin
- 1 tsp smoked paprika
- salt and freshly ground black pepper
- 100 g/3½ oz quinoa
- 1 chicken stock cube (optional)
- handful of flat-leaf parsley, chopped
- zest and juice of 1 lemon
- small handful coriander/cilantro, roughly chopped
- 100 g/3½ oz pomegranate seeds
- 40 g/1½ oz pistachios, roughly chopped

1. Preheat the oven to 210°C/190°C fan/gas mark 6.
2. Put the cauliflower on a baking tray and drizzle with 2 tbsp of the olive oil, then toss with the cumin and paprika. Season with salt and pepper.
3. Bake for 20–25 minutes, until the florets are golden and just cooked but not soft. Leave to cool.
4. Put the quinoa in a saucepan with plenty of water – you can add a chicken stock cube for flavor if you wish. Cook on a medium heat for 15–18 minutes. Drain any excess water.
5. Mix the cooked quinoa with the parsley, lemon juice and zest, remaining olive oil and coriander. Divide the dressed quinoa between two jars, then add a layer of pomegranate seeds, followed by the roasted cauliflower and pistachios scattered on top.

Spicy Sichuan ginger prawns

Serves 4

Gingerol, found in ginger, has been shown to induce anti-inflammatory responses in obesity-linked metabolic disorders. Prawns/shrimp contain zinc, essential for immune function, as well as astaxanthin, a potent antioxidant.

Sauce

- 1 tbsp tomato purée
- 3 tbsp chilli bean paste
- 2 tsp rice wine vinegar
- 2 tbsp maple syrup
- 1 tsp sesame oil

- 1 tbsp flaxseed or coconut oil
- 2 cm/¾ in piece of fresh ginger, peeled and finely sliced

- 2 garlic cloves, peeled and finely sliced
- 1 spring onion/scallion, finely sliced
- 450 g/16 oz raw prawns/shrimp
- Coriander/cilantro leaves, to serve.

1. To make the sauce, mix all the ingredients together in a small bowl and set aside.
2. Heat the flaxseed or coconut oil in a wok and fry the ginger, garlic and spring onion for 1 minute. Add the prawns and stir-fry for 1 more minute. Carefully add the sauce and continue cooking for 2 more minutes.
3. Tip the prawns onto serving plates and scatter with the coriander leaves. This dish is delicious served with courgettini (courgettes/zucchini that have been spiralized) or brown/wild rice.

Chicken satay with spicy peanut dipping sauce

Serves 4

Peanuts are a multipurpose legume and contain substantial amounts of resveratrol and quercetin. They have shown promising results in clinical trials for lowering blood glucose.

Dipping sauce
- 250 g/9 oz peanut butter
- 2 garlic cloves, peeled and crushed
- 1 tbsp fresh ginger
- 1 tsp grated or ground turmeric
- 1 tsp Tabasco
- 1 tbsp sesame oil
- 4 tbsp soy sauce

- 2 tbsp clear honey
- juice of 1 lemon

- 4 tbsp soy sauce
- 2 tbsp mirin
- 4 tbsp sake
- 1 tbsp dark maple syrup
- 8 boneless chicken thighs

1. To make the dipping sauce, put all the ingredients in a blender with 125 ml/4 fl oz/½ cup water and blitz. Set aside.
2. Put all the other ingredients except the chicken into a saucepan and simmer for about 5 minutes – watch it carefully so it doesn't all evaporate! Allow this marinade to cool.
3. Cut each chicken thigh into 3 even pieces, coat with the marinade and leave covered in the fridge for a couple of hours. When ready to cook, thread the chicken onto 4 skewers.
4. Cook on a griddle pan over a medium heat for 5–6 minutes each side.
5. Serve with the dipping sauce, rice and broccoli.

Asparagus roasted with garlic and sesame seeds

Serves 4

Allicin in garlic has anti-inflammatory properties, and asparagus is high in folate and vitamins A, C and K. Sesame seeds are packed with calcium, potassium, magnesium and vitamin B6.

- 2 large bunches of asparagus, woody ends removed
- 1 tbsp sesame oil
- 1 tbsp toasted sesame seeds
- salt and freshly ground black pepper
- 3 garlic cloves, peeled and crushed

1. Preheat the oven to 200°C/180°C fan/gas mark 6.
2. Place the asparagus in a bowl and toss with the sesame oil, sesame seeds and garlic. Season with salt and pepper.
3. Spread the asparagus on a baking tray and roast in the oven for 20 minutes.
4. Serve immediately.

Black bean chocolate chilli

Serves 4

Dark chocolate is a delicious way to increase your intake of antioxidants. This recipe is also great for detoxification.

- 2 tbsp olive oil
- 1 onion, peeled and sliced
- 2 red peppers/red bell peppers, finely sliced
- 4 field mushrooms, thickly sliced
- 2 garlic cloves, peeled and finely sliced
- 1 tbsp mild chilli powder
- 1 tsp chipotle paste
- 1 tbsp maple syrup
- 1 tbsp ground cumin
- 1 tbsp ground coriander/cilantro
- 2 x 400 g/14 oz tins black beans, drained
- 2 x 400 g/14 oz boxes or bottles chopped tomatoes
- 150 ml/5 fl oz/½ cup + 2 tbsp vegetable stock
- 15 g/½ oz 85% dark chocolate
- salt and freshly ground black pepper
- 150 ml/5 fl oz/½ cup + 2 tbsp sour cream or Greek yogurt, to serve
- 150 g/5½ oz feta, to serve
- coriander/cilantro leaves, finely chopped, to serve
- lime wedges, to serve

1. Heat the olive oil in a large pan and cook the onion and peppers for about 10 minutes until softened. Add the mushrooms and garlic and cook for a further few minutes.
2. Add the chilli powder and chipotle paste, maple syrup, cumin and coriander and stir to coat everything thoroughly. Add the beans and chopped tomatoes, then add 100 ml/3½ fl oz/7 tbsp of the stock and bring to a simmering boil. Add the chocolate and stir until it melts. Season and simmer for 30 minutes. If the liquid reduces too much, add a little more stock.
3. Adjust the seasoning and serve with sour cream or yogurt, feta, coriander, lime and Spicy mango guacamole (see below).

Spicy mango guacamole

Serves 4

Avocados are an ideal source of monounsaturated fatty acids (MUFAs) folate, vitamin B, soluble fibre, vitamin E, copper and potassium.

- 2 large ripe avocados, cut into small pieces
- 1 fresh mango, finely cubed
- ½ red onion, peeled and very finely chopped
- juice of 1 lime
- 1 garlic clove, crushed
- 1 tbsp olive oil
- pinch of salt and freshly ground black pepper
- 1 red chilli, deseeded and finely chopped

1. Mix all the ingredients in a small bowl – then please taste! It may need more lime, salt or garlic depending on how you like it.

Beetroot tzatziki

Serves 4

Beetroot gets its colour from anthocyanin, a potent antioxidant. It is also high in dietary nitrates, which can lower blood pressure. Not only that, but beets are high in fibre, folate, potassium, and vitamin C. Manganese in beetroot plays an important role as a cofactor (helper molecule) in oxidative stress metabolism.

- 2 small beetroot/beet, cooked and grated
- 125 ml/4 fl oz/½ cup Greek yogurt
- 1 tbsp fresh dill, finely chopped
- 1 small garlic clove, crushed
- 1 tsp red wine vinegar
- 1 tsp of olive oil
- salt and freshly ground black pepper

1. Preheat the oven to 200°C/180°C fan/gas mark 6.
2. Wrap each beetroot bulb (with the skin on) in kitchen foil or greaseproof paper and roast in the oven for 1 hour.
3. When cool, unwrap the beetroot and the skin will peel away if you rub it gently.
4. To make the tzatziki, combine the beetroot, yogurt, dill and garlic. Add the vinegar, oil and salt and pepper, to taste. Cover and chill for 30 minutes in the fridge to allow the flavours to blend.

Tip: I suggest using a pair of rubber gloves to handle the beetroot – this will stop you looking like you've just come away from a murder scene!

Brazil nut and tarragon pesto

Serves 4

Brazil nuts are a brilliant source of selenium and monounsaturated fatty acids (MUFAs). Selenium is an essential cofactor for the proper functioning of our antioxidant system which protects our cells. Calcium, zinc, potassium, manganese, phosphorus and iron – also found in Brazil nuts – are all essential minerals for optimal health.

- handful of flat-leaf parsley
- 6 large Brazil nuts, coarsely chopped
- 1 tbsp tarragon, chopped
- 1 large garlic clove, chopped
- ½ tsp finely grated lemon zest
- 5 tbsp extra-virgin olive oil
- 2 tbsp freshly grated Parmesan cheese
- salt and freshly ground black pepper

1. In a mini food processor, combine the parsley with the Brazil nuts, 2 tbsp water, tarragon, garlic and lemon zest and pulse to a coarse paste.
2. Add 3 tbsp of the olive oil and the Parmesan and process to a slightly smooth paste, adding more oil if needed.
3. Season with salt and pepper, to taste.

Mexican quinoa salad with orange and lime dressing

Serves 4

Quinoa is a gluten-free source of protein and fibre. It contains manganese and magnesium, minerals essential for many metabolic functions. It is also a good source of amino acids and, due to the high fibre, is a low-GI grain.

The glycaemic index (GI) of a food indicates how rapidly the carbohydrate you are eating is digested and released as glucose into the bloodstream, thus raising (spiking) blood sugar levels. The hormone insulin is released from the pancreas in order to reduce the level of glucose in the bloodstream. If this balance is not kept in check, insulin resistance results.

The GI scale is measured as 1–100, and low GI is preferable for average everyday activity.

Another very important aspect to consider is the glycaemic load of a food.

The glycaemic load (GL) identifies the amount of carbohydrate in a food source as well as the quality of the food, whereas the GI is only a measure of the influence of the food source on blood sugar levels. For example, the GI of a slice of watermelon is 72 (high) but the GL is only 7 (low). This is because watermelon has a high fluid content and contains high amounts of fibre, antioxidants and minerals, which are all highly beneficial to your health.

- 1 x 160 g/5½ oz bag mixed salad leaves
- 150 g/5½ oz cooked quinoa (red or white)
- 1 x 165 g/5¾ oz small tin drained sweetcorn/corn
- ½ 400 g/14 oz tin black beans, drained and rinsed
- ½ red onion, peeled and finely sliced
- 1 orange, segmented
- ½ ripe avocado, chopped
- handful of chopped coriander/cilantro

Dressing
- juice of 1 large lime
- juice of 1 orange
- 2 tsp maple syrup
- 1 tsp Tabasco
- 1 tsp chipotle paste
- pinch each of sea salt and freshly ground black pepper
- 3–4 tbsp extra virgin olive oil

1. Put all the salad ingredients in a large bowl and toss them together.
2. Put the dressing ingredients in a jar with a lid and shake to combine.
3. Dress the salad and serve.

Drinks

Chocolate, banana and peanut milkshake

Serves 1

Dark chocolate is high in magnesium and is an awesome anti-inflammatory ingredient. Bananas also contain magnesium, manganese, potassium, fibre – both soluble and insoluble – and vitamin B6 and vitamin C. Peanuts contain the antioxidant quercetin. Peanuts have also been shown to reduce blood sugar levels in individuals with type 2 diabetes risk.

- 240 ml/8 fl oz/1 cup dark chocolate almond milk
- 1 banana
- 1 tbsp peanut butter
- 7–8 ice cubes

1. Put all the ingredients in a jug and blitz with a blender. Serve at once.

Cashew nut and cinnamon milk

Serves 4

Cashew nuts contain iron, magnesium, zinc, copper, phosphorus and manganese. Cinnamon has shown some potential to help control pre-diabetic and diabetic conditions.

- 250 g raw cashews
- 750 ml/26 fl oz/3¼ cups chilled water
- 1–2 tbsp maple syrup or honey
- 2 tsp vanilla extract
- dash of sea salt
- pinch of cinnamon

1. Start by soaking the cashew nuts in water 4 hours before you want your drink.
2. Drain and add ½ of the chilled water and blitz with a blender. Slowly add the remaining water and the other ingredients, and blitz again.
3. Taste and adjust the seasoning to your personal preference. If you like your milk slightly less thick, add more water.

Tip: This drink can be stored in the fridge for up to 3 days, but it may need a little stir. Serve cold.

Chapter 4

Detoxification

Detoxification is *not* a 'cleansing' diet, a handful of laxatives or a matter of 'sweating it out'. It is a full service – a demanding job that operates 24/7.

Detoxification takes place primarily in the liver. The liver plays many vital roles in our bodies, and most of our organs rely on it to keep things neat and tidy. Our liver is responsible for 'cleaning' everything we swallow, breathe in, and even touch. It is responsible for filtering blood and neutralizing toxins that come in many forms. Alcohol, caffeine and fatty foods usually spring to mind, but there are also all the medications we swallow, pesticides in our food supply, pollution, household detergents, room sprays, lotions, plastics in our food containers, and chemicals and toxins in our drinking water. Our oceans are littered with plastics and heavy metals and we can't possibly avoid them all. Our bodies also produce hormones and waste products of oxidative stress that our liver has to detoxify. It's a very high-risk job!

The modern diet is a combination of harmful substances as well as protective nutrients that most of us try to eat.

Xenobiotics (harmful substances) come in many forms that are difficult to avoid and we are exposed to a multitude of them during our lifetimes. These include food additives, pharmaceuticals and environmental pollutants. As individuals, we vary in the amount of chemicals we are exposed to (depending on where we live, the food we eat, the type of job we do) and our individual genetic profile also determines how efficiently our liver can detoxify these substances.

The detoxification process takes part in two phases (see Figure 4.1) and we are equipped with enzymes that deal with Phase 1 and Phase 2. A simplified version of this complex process involves Phase 1 'activators' and Phase 2 'excretors'.

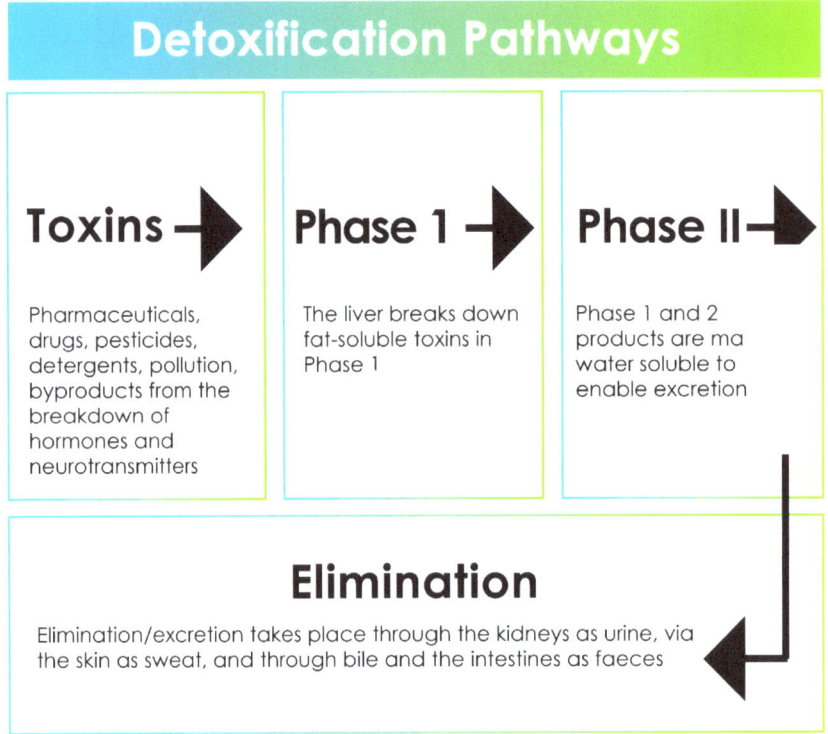

Figure 4.1: Detoxification pathways

Cruciferous and allium vegetables

Of all the fruit and vegetables that we need to eat to keep healthy and protect ourselves from cancer and other illnesses, cruciferous vegetables (also known as *Brassica* vegetables) and allium vegetables are the heroes. Scientific evidence has shown that eating cruciferous and allium vegetables helps to increase the activity of crucial detoxification genes and enzymes. Molecules found in broccoli and other cruciferous vegetables activate the Nrf2 pathway, which in turn activates our internal defence system which works tirelessly to protect us from many diseases.

Cruciferous vegetables are named for their cross-shaped flowers. They all contain substances called glucosinolates. Allium vegetables contain a substance called allicin. Garlic is particularly high in allicin (see Table 4.1). Research has found that garlic, onions and leeks may reduce the incidence of stomach and bowel cancer.

Table 4.1: Some examples of cruciferous and allium vegetables to add to your toolbox

Cruciferous vegetables	Allium vegetables
Eat these: broccoli, cauliflower, Brussels sprouts, cabbage, watercress, bok choy, kale, radishes, horseradish, daikon radish, wasabi and turnips	*Eat these:* onions, spring onions/scallions, shallots, garlic, leeks and chives

How much is enough?

We should all be eating cruciferous and allium vegetables at least four times a week, but some people may need to increase their intake even more. One serving of onions, garlic, chives or leeks per day will assist with Phase 1 detoxification, and at least one serving of (preferably raw) broccoli, cauliflower, cabbage, Brussels sprouts or watercress per day is also recommended for Phase 1 detoxification. Eating cruciferous and allium vegetables daily supports liver detoxification because Phase 1 detoxification impacts Phase 2 detoxification. If there's a hold-up in the system at the first phase, the toxic load is increased when it comes to the second phase. Just as traffic flow on the motorway builds up if there's at a hitch at junction 1, junction 2 gets backed up too. By supporting Phase 1 enzymes, the toxic load will be reduced for Phase 2 enzymes and detoxification is increased. The upside of having slower Phase 2 detoxification is that if you are eating sufficient cruciferous vegetables, the slower detoxification results in the good stuff remaining in the bloodstream for longer. Unfortunately, the bad stuff like toxins also hang around too long and are possibly not excreted effectively.

There is very strong evidence that these wonderful crunchy veggies (broccoli in particular) help to prevent cancer. The active ingredient in broccoli (sulphoraphane) and the myrosinase enzyme that is produced when we crunch into it is destroyed by heat. For this reason, most of the recipes that follow in this section use raw broccoli. If you are going to cook your broccoli, try not to steam it for more than 2–3 minutes.

Fermented foods

For all the complex detoxification processes to occur, a healthy gut and an acid–alkali balance is needed. Elimination in our bodies needs to take place via urine and faeces, and constipation will definitely hold up the process. That is why fibre from plant sources and gut-healing, fermented foods are so important in the diet.

Certain ancient foods have made a comeback due to their ability to reintroduce a variety of gut microbes that were previously lost as a result of the modern Western diet. Fermented plant products such as miso, kefir, kombucha, natto, kimchi and fermented olives provide fibre, bioactive polyphenols, vitamins, minerals and lactic acid bacteria, which will all help to keep your gut healthy and assist your liver with its daily task of keeping you energized and thriving.

Fermentation also produces secondary phytochemicals which have been shown to benefit not only the antioxidant process, but also chronic conditions such as obesity, type 2 diabetes, cholesterol metabolism, cardiovascular disease, IBD and some mental health disorders. Because we all differ in our billions of gut bacteria, some individuals with IBS, may find that they do not respond well to fermented foods. In some circumstances, it's advisable to investigate further via stool testing in order to establish imbalances in commensal bacteria.

How much is a serving of fruit and veg?

'Back in the day', one serving of meat and three servings of veg per day were perfectly acceptable, but now that the recommended daily serving of fruit and vegetables has gone from 5 to 10, many people worry about how you can fit it all in! However, there is still room for the meat (or lentils) – a serving of fruit and veg is often far less than you might imagine (see Table 4.2).

Table 4.2: Serving sizes for fruit and veg

One serving of fruit	One serving of vegetables
1 medium apple or ½ large apple	1 carrot
½ peach	6 green beans
½ avocado	1 sweet potato
1 kiwi fruit or 2 small kiwi fruit	1 baked potato
½ grapefruit	2 long broccoli spears or 120 ml/½ cup of raw chopped broccoli
1 small banana	120 ml/½ cup of Brussels sprouts
180 ml/¾ cup of berries	240 ml/1 cup of kale or spinach
120 ml/½ cup of fruit salad	240 ml/1 cup of salad leaves
240 ml/1 cup of cubed watermelon or 2 wedges	120 ml/½ cup of chopped red or white cabbage
½ cup of fresh pineapple chunks	120 ml/½ bell pepper
1 heaped tbsp of dried cranberries	120 ml/½ cup of cauliflower or 7 florets
3 dried preservative-free apricots	120 ml/½ cup of bok choy
½ pear	1 medium tomato or 8 vine baby tomatoes or 30 g/1 oz tomato purée
2 small plums	
32 (small bunch) red or black grapes	

Your Healing Kitchen

Ingredients known to support detoxification include: Brussel sprouts, cress, turnips, Savoy cabbage, kale, watercress, kohlrabi, red cabbage, broccoli, horseradish, wasabi, bok choy, garlic, onions, leeks, radishes, tofu, miso, kimchi, kombucha, liquorice root supplements, flaxseeds, grains, brown rice, lentils, oats, barley, buckwheat.

Fast food

- Packet of radishes
- Bag of raw crunchy broccoli dipped in hummus
- Sushi or sashimi with lots of wasabi and ginger
- Egg and cress sandwich on seeded brown soda bread (try to avoid supermarket 'sliced loaves')
- Pickled onions
- Grilled chicken salad with coleslaw (check the label – preferably no vegetable oil)
- 2 squares of 85% dark chocolate

Easy recipes

BREAKFAST

Spinach, salmon and feta hot cakes
Rainbow fruit platter with yogurt and honey
Overnight spiced apple oats

MAIN MEALS

SPA (spinach, prawn and avocado) salad
Blackened miso and ginger
marinated cod with steamed spinach
Debbi's raw broccoli, avocado, feta and mint salad
Garlic roasted chicken
(served with Broccoli and miso mustard dressing)
Aloo-gobi (cauliflower, turmeric,
pea and onion curry)
Wasabi-crusted cod
(served with Apple and lemon coleslaw)
Sauerkraut
Stuffed feta, walnut and parsley roast onions
with a simple green salad
Roast cauliflower nuggets with green chilli pesto
Spicy sea bass with a crispy skin
Creamy sprout and leek colcannon
with pan-fried calf's liver

TREATS

Spiced Earl Grey tea loaf

DRINKS

Mexican chilli hot chocolate
Mo-tea-to mocktail
Green smoothie

Breakfast

Spinach, salmon and feta hot cakes

Serves 2

Onion (an allium vegetable) supports Phase 1 detoxification pathways and contains quercetin which is anti-inflammatory and may support the immune system by preventing the release of histamine (chemicals that cause allergic reactions). Spinach contains lutein (good for eye health) and folate (good for methylation and multiple antioxidants).

- 250 g/9 oz fresh baby spinach
- 1 tbsp olive oil
- 1 spring onion/scallion, finely sliced
- 50 g/1¾ oz wholemeal/wholewheat flour
- 1 large organic egg
- ½ tsp ground cumin
- 25 g/1 oz feta cheese, crumbled
- 2 slices of smoked salmon

1. Put the spinach in a saucepan with ½ tbsp of olive oil and cook for 3 minutes, stirring constantly until the spinach has wilted and reduced in volume. Cool, then roughly chop.
2. Mix in all the other ingredients, except the remaining oil.
3. Now, using your hands, shape the mixture into 2 cakes (about 10 cm/4 in wide and 1 cm/½ in high).
4. Heat the remaining oil in the frying pan and cook the cakes for 3 minutes on each side, using a spatula to carefully flip them over once during cooking.
5. Serve with more smoked salmon, scrambled eggs or 2 tbsp of live yogurt.

Rainbow fruit platter with yogurt and honey

Serves 2

This fruity rainbow is rich in antioxidants and digestive enzymes to put a little 'vroom' in your engine and support many biological functions. Kiwi fruit is particularly high in vitamin C, which is essential for a healthy immune system and performs multiple functions within our cells. Oranges contain folate, even though they are not green!

If you can source all these fruits, the result is spectacular. If it seems excessive, the best nutrigenomic ingredients for detoxification are pineapple, orange and pomegranate seeds. Use this recipe to support oxidative stress and methylation as well.

- handful of raspberries
- handful of pomegranate seeds
- handful of melon slices
- handful of orange segments
- handful of pineapple slices
- handful of papaya slices
- handful of kiwi slices
- handful of blueberries
- handful of red grapes

To serve
- 1 heaped tbsp probiotic yogurt
- 1 tsp Manuka honey

1. Peel and slice the fruit as required and arrange it on a large serving plate – if you're slightly obsessive, as I am, arrange it in rainbow colour order.
2. Drizzle the honey over the yogurt and serve with the fruit.

Overnight spiced apple oats

Serves 2

An apple a day really does help to keep the doctor away! There really isn't enough space to list all the health benefits of apples, but, importantly, they contain phenolics and flavonoids and quercetin. The seeds and nuts provide essential minerals such as magnesium, manganese and selenium, which act as cofactors to support oxidative stress. Vitamin D and calcium (found in most nuts and seeds) are important for bone health and cardiovascular health.

- 1 eating apple, coarsely grated
- 50 g/1¾ oz organic porridge oats/rolled oats
- 25 g/1 oz mixed seeds (e.g. sunflower, pumpkin, sesame and linseed)
- 25 g/1 oz mixed nuts (e.g. Brazils, hazelnuts, almonds, pecans and walnuts), roughly chopped
- ¼ tsp ground cinnamon
- 100 g/3½ oz full-fat, plain bio-yogurt (yogurt with live cultures)
- 25 g/1 oz organic sultanas

1. Put the grated apple in a bowl and add the oats, seeds, half the nuts and the cinnamon. Toss together well.
2. Stir in the yogurt and 100 ml/3½ fl oz/7 tbsp cold water, then cover and chill in the fridge for several hours or overnight.
3. Serve the muesli topped with the sultanas and remaining nuts.

Main meals

SPA (spinach, prawn and avocado) salad

Serves 2

Prawns/shrimp are a great source of astaxanthin. This antioxidant is brilliant for our skin and oxidative stress, and is also great for methylation and inflammation.

- ½ red chilli, deseeded and finely sliced
- 1 small garlic clove, finely chopped
- finely grated zest and juice of 1 lime
- 1 tbsp soy sauce
- 1 tbsp sesame oil
- 100 g/3½ oz large prawns/shrimp, peeled and cooked
- 140 g/5 oz baby spinach
- 1 avocado

1. In a large bowl mix together the chilli, garlic, lime zest and juice, soy sauce and sesame oil, then add the prawns and toss to coat. You can leave the prawns to marinate, covered, in the fridge for an hour or so.
2. Lift the prawns out of the marinade. Toss the spinach in the marinade until coated, then transfer the spinach to a serving dish.
3. Slice the avocado and tuck the prawns and pieces of avocado in amongst the spinach.

Blackened miso and ginger marinated cod with steamed spinach

Serves 4

Cod contains omega-3 fatty acids and is high in protein. Miso is fermented soy paste, which helps to nourish commensal bacteria within the gut and therefore plays an important part in the detoxification process. Ginger is a potent anti-inflammatory ingredient. Spinach is high in folate and is vital for methylation, which is linked to detoxification.

Marinade
- 4 tbsp white miso paste
- 6 tbsp sake
- 2 garlic cloves, peeled and finely grated
- 10 g/¼ oz fresh ginger root, peeled and finely grated
- 1 tbsp maple syrup
- 1 tbsp rice wine vinegar

- 4 x 200 g/7 oz cod fillets, skin on
- 2 tbsp rapeseed/canola oil
- bag of fresh baby spinach leaves
- 2 limes, quartered, to serve

1. Mix all the marinade ingredients together in a large bowl, then add the cod. Cover and marinade for 2 days in the fridge.
2. Preheat the oven to 220°C/200°C fan/gas mark 7.
3. Heat the oil in a large, ovenproof frying pan. Drain the cod, then put the fillets skin side down in the pan and cook on high heat for 3 minutes. Carefully flip the fish over and cook for a further 3 minutes. Put the pan in the oven for 6 minutes.
4. Wilt the spinach in a saucepan with a splash of olive oil for 1 minute, then serve alongside the cod, with a squeeze of lime.

Tip: The miso marinade can be used on other white fish and organic chicken breasts.

Debbi's raw broccoli, avocado, feta and mint salad

Serves 2

We can't stress enough how wonderful raw broccoli is! Research shows that it may be protective against certain cancers. Although sulphoraphane (found in broccoli and cauliflower) is a natural insecticide and toxic to tiny caterpillars, it isn't dangerous for us large humans!

Vinaigrette
- 1 tbsp maple syrup
- 2 tbsp apple cider vinegar
- 3 tbsp olive oil

- 1 small head of broccoli, cut into bitesize florets
- 120 g/4¼ oz freshly cooked peas
- ½ cucumber, deseeded and sliced
- 100 g/3½ oz crumbled feta
- small avocado, chopped
- 1 small handful of flat leaf parsley, chopped
- handful of mint, chopped
- 100 g/3½ oz cooked quinoa (as per packet instructions)

1. Shake all the vinaigrette ingredients together with some seasoning in a jar with a lid until combined.
2. Put the salad ingredients in a big salad bowl, pour the vinaigrette over the salad and toss before serving.

Garlic roasted chicken

Serves 4

Garlic is an important activator of Phase 1 detoxification and has been used to treat many ailments since biblical times. Its enzyme, allicin, is a powerful antifungal. Choline (found in chicken) can offer additional support for methylation. Rosmarinic acid (found in rosemary) is a polyphenol with anti-inflammatory and anti-allergy benefits; it can also be used for oxidative stress.

- 4 large chicken legs
- 2 garlic bulbs (approximately 20 cloves), peeled
- 6 shallots cut in half, outer skins removed
- 1 organic lemon, cut into 8 segments
- 2 tbsp fresh rosemary, finely chopped
- 2 tbsp thyme, chopped
- 4 tbsp good-quality olive oil
- 150 ml/7 fl oz/¾ cup + 2 tbsp chicken stock
- salt and freshly ground black pepper

1. Preheat the oven to 200°C/180°C fan/gas mark 6.
2. Put the chicken, skin side up, in a large roasting pan. Tuck the garlic, shallots, lemons and herbs around the chicken, then pour the olive oil and the chicken stock over the other ingredients in the pan. Season generously with salt and pepper.
3. Cover loosely with kitchen foil and roast in the oven for 1 hour.
4. After 1 hour, turn the heat up to 220°C/200°C fan/gas mark 7, remove the foil and cook for a further 30 minutes.
5. Serve with Broccoli and miso mustard dressing (see below).

Tip: Use leftover roast chicken to make a chicken salad or add to an organic stock cube and boiling water plus a handful of baby spinach leaves to make a warming, quick chicken soup.

Broccoli and miso mustard dressing

Serves 4

Myrosinase is an essential enzyme in broccoli. However, it doesn't like heat and is destroyed at high temperatures or when microwaved. A super-quick blanching is therefore advised in this recipe!

Dressing
- ½ tsp Dijon mustard
- 2 tbsp miso (white or brown)
- 1 tbsp clear honey
- 1½ tbsp rice vinegar
- 1 large head of broccoli, cut into florets
- handful of sesame seeds, to serve

1. Put all the dressing ingredients in a jar with a lid and shake until combined – you may need a splash of water to loosen it.
2. Blanch the broccoli in boiling water for 2 minutes.
3. Pour the dressing over the broccoli and scatter the sesame seeds on top.
4. Serve with Garlic roasted chicken (see above).

Aloo-gobi
(cauliflower, turmeric, pea and onion curry)

Serves 4

Cauliflower is a rich source of vitamin B, choline, folate, manganese, vitamin K, vitamin C and potassium. This cruciferous vegetable is useful for Phase 2 detoxification.

- 3 tbsp olive oil (or rapeseed/canola oil if you prefer)
- 1 white onion, peeled and diced
- 3 garlic cloves, peeled and crushed
- 1 large sweet potato, peeled and cut into 1 cm/½ in cubes
- ½ head of cauliflower, separated into 2 cm/¾ in florets
- 1 tsp ground cumin
- ½ tsp ground coriander/cilantro
- ½ tsp ground turmeric
- ½ tsp garam masala
- ½ tsp fennel seeds, coarsely ground
- 1 tsp salt
- 50 g/1¾/3½ oz frozen peas
- 1 tsp fresh lemon juice
- 1 tbsp Greek probiotic yogurt
- Coriander/cilantro leaves, chopped, to serve

1. Heat the oil in a large pan. Fry the onion and garlic for 4 minutes on a medium heat, then add the sweet potato and stir briskly for 1 minute. Add the cauliflower, spices, fennel seeds and salt, stirring to coat everything. Now add 3 tbsp water, turn down the heat and cook for 8–10 minutes, covered, until both the sweet potato and the cauliflower are tender (add a little more water if necessary). Add the peas, lemon juice and yogurt and cook for a further 2 minutes.
2. Serve sprinkled with chopped coriander leaves.

Wasabi-crusted cod

Serves 2

Wasabi and garlic support the detoxification process, and cod is an ideal source of protein.

Crust
- 1 shallot, finely diced
- 4 tbsp flaked almonds/sliced almonds
- 1 garlic clove, crushed
- 1 tsp wasabi paste
- handful of coriander/cilantro, chopped
- juice of ½ lime
- 2 cod fillets (or hake)

1. Preheat the oven to 200°C/180°C fan/gas mark 6.
2. Put all the crust ingredients in a bowl and mix to form a paste. Smear 1 tbsp of the crust mixture over the cod fillets and put them in an ovenproof dish. Add 2 tbsp cold water to stop the fish sticking and cook for 17 minutes.
3. Serve with Apple and lemon coleslaw (see below).

Apple and lemon coleslaw

Serves 4

Cabbage is a fabulous sulphur-containing vegetable and supports Phase 2 detoxification, but is often sidelined in favour of so-called 'superfoods'. Cabbage is a hero that is simple and easy to prepare. Coleslaw is the ultimate combo for detoxification. Apple and carrot contribute to the antioxidant boost that we all need.

- ¼ red cabbage, very finely shredded
- ¼ white cabbage, very finely shredded
- 1 red apple, grated
- 1 carrot, grated
- handful of fresh mint
- 4 heaped tbsp mayonnaise (homemade is best – see Speedy mayonnaise below)
- squeeze of lemon juice
- salt and freshly ground black pepper

1. Mix all the ingredients together in a bowl. Season with salt and pepper, to taste.
2. Serve with Wasabi-crusted cod (see above).

Speedy mayonnaise

This mayo is high in choline and ideal for enhancing methylation. Olive oil is the doctor on call for everything!

- 2 tsp lemon juice
- 1 large whole egg (at room temperature)
- ½ tsp dried mustard powder
- 250 ml/9 fl oz/1 cup + 2 tbsp olive oil
- salt

1. Put the lemon juice, the egg, mustard and finally the oil in a large mug or tall, narrow measuring jug. Let the ingredients rest for 20 seconds.
2. Push a handheld blender all the way to the bottom of the container. Turn it on to high speed and leave it at the bottom of the container for about 20 seconds.
3. Now, slowly pull the blender towards the top of the container without taking the blades out of the mayonnaise.
4. Now push it back towards the bottom of the container. Repeat this step a couple of times until all the ingredients are well incorporated.
5. Add salt, to taste.

Sauerkraut

Makes enough to fill 3 x 475 ml/16 oz jars

Fermented foods are really, really good for your gut health! This is a relatively easy recipe, albeit rather time-consuming (but well worth the effort). If you don't want to faff about with sterilizing jars and waiting 10 days, bought sauerkraut isn't a bad alternative. Use natural, organic sauerkraut from a reputable supplier because 'bought' sauerkraut is not the same fermentation process due to the addition of sugar and vinegar.

- 1 large red cabbage, finely grated
- 1½–2 tsp sea salt
- 1 small raw beetroot/beet, washed and finely grated (no need to peel)
- 3 whole carrots, peeled and finely grated
- 3 tbsp fresh turmeric, grated
- 3 tbsp fresh ginger, grated
- 4 garlic cloves, peeled and crushed

1. Sterilize any equipment you are about to use and let it dry completely (put everything in the sink and cover with boiling water, then allow to come to room temperature).
2. Put the cabbage in a large mixing bowl, add 1½ tsp of salt and massage the cabbage with your hands for about 5 minutes. During this time a lot of liquid will come out of the cabbage and the volume of cabbage will appear to shrink.
3. Now add the beetroot, carrot, turmeric, ginger and garlic. Wash your hands again and continue to massage the slaw.
4. Using your hands, put the slaw into the sterilized jars and push down firmly to pack in the mixture. Leave about ¼ of the jar empty, to allow for some expansion when the slaw begins to ferment. There should be sufficient liquid to cover the cabbage mixture (but if there isn't, top up with boiled water).

5. Fermentation should begin to happen within 24 hours. Store in a dark place away from sunlight and preferably somewhere fairly warm (about 18°C).

Tip: I reckon the best slaw is ready after about 10 days, but each day open the jars and, using sterilized utensils, give it a little mix and make sure the cabbage is still covered in liquid.

After 10 days, move the jars to the fridge. The sauerkraut will be delicious for up to 3 months (the longer you leave it, the more tangy it becomes).

Sauerkraut is usually served as an accompaniment to cold chicken or leftover beef.

Stuffed feta, walnut and parsley roast onions with a simple green salad

Serves 2

Parsley contains high amounts of vitamin C and folate. Vitamin C is vital for immune function, adrenal glands, detoxification, bone health and collagen formation, recovery from illness and exercise. Folate is needed in the methylation cycle, which is essential for DNA replication and repair in order to reduce the risk of cancer and other diseases.

- 2 medium onions, peeled
- 1 slice wholemeal/wholewheat or sourdough bread, crumbed
- 2 tbsp olive oil + extra for greasing
- 1 garlic clove, crushed
- 75 g/2½ oz feta cheese, crumbled
- handful of walnuts, chopped
- small handful of parsley, finely chopped
- Freshly ground black pepper

1. Preheat the oven to 200°C/180°C fan/gas mark 6.
2. Cut a small slice off the top and bottom of the onions and discard the slices. Place the onions in a pan of water and bring to the boil, then lower the heat and simmer gently for 10 minutes. Remove the onions with a slotted spoon and cool slightly. When they are cool enough to handle, remove and chop the inner sections of the onions, leaving about 3 outer layers. Put the outer layers of the onions in a greased oven dish.
3. Fry the breadcrumbs in the oil with the garlic and inner onion sections for about 5 minutes – the breadcrumbs should be slightly golden. Add the feta, walnuts and parsley. Mix gently, then spoon this mixture into the outer sections of the onions. Season with black pepper – there is no need to use salt as the feta is quite salty. Bake in the oven for 25 minutes.
4. Serve with green salad, plus one of the dressings from 'Great easy salad dressings to store in the fridge' in Chapter 1.

Roast cauliflower nuggets with green chilli pesto

Serves 4

Allicin in garlic can help reduce the risk of cancer and has been shown to be protective against blood clots. Cauliflower, as we have already mentioned, performs a great job in supporting Phase 2 detoxification. It is also great for methylation, oxidative stress and inflammation.

- 1 large cauliflower, cut into medium florets
- 2 tbsp olive oil
- 2 cloves garlic, crushed
- 2 tsp fresh, grated turmeric
- 3 tsp cumin powder
- 3 tsp ground coriander/cilantro
- 1 tsp salt
- handful of roughly chopped coriander/cilantro
- handful of roughly chopped parsley

Pesto
- 1 large handful of fresh coriander/cilantro
- 60 g/2¼ oz cashew nuts or peanuts
- 1 garlic clove, roughly chopped
- zest and juice of ½ large lemon
- pinch of salt
- 2 tsp white wine vinegar or lemon juice
- 1 tsp maple syrup
- 1 small green chilli
- 1 tbsp water

1. Preheat the oven to 220°C/200°C fan/gas mark 7.
2. Put the cauliflower, oil, garlic, spices and salt in a large bowl and mix well, using your hands. Now put the spicy cauliflower nuggets in a roasting pan and cook for 40 minutes, until the cauliflower is cooked through and charred around the edges.
3. To make the pesto, put all the ingredients in a small food processor or blender. Blitz until you have your desired consistency – the sauce should still have some texture. If it is too thick, you can always add more water.
4. Put the roasted cauliflower on a serving plate and spoon the pesto over it.

Spicy sea bass with a crispy skin

Serves 2

Garlic and spring onions support detoxification and ginger is good for 'everything'. If you are avoiding heavy metals such as mercury, use salmon, cod or hake instead of sea bass. Unfortunately, our oceans and large fish such as tuna, sea bass, marlin and sword fish contain high levels of mercury. Mercury and other heavy metals (lead, arsenic, cadmium, thallium, bismuth) impact detoxification and affect methylation genes as well.

- 2 large sea bass fillets
- 2 tbsp olive oil
- 20 g/¾ oz knob ginger root, peeled and finely sliced into matchsticks
- 1 garlic clove, peeled and thinly sliced
- 1 red chilli, deseeded and thinly shredded
- 2 spring onions/scallions, finely sliced
- 1 tbsp soy sauce

1. Season the fish, then slash the skin three times using a sharp knife.
2. Heat a heavy-based frying pan and add 1 tbsp oil. Once hot, fry the fish skin side down for 4 minutes until the skin is very crisp and golden. The fish will be almost cooked through. Turn it over, cook for another 30 seconds, then remove fish onto a serving plate.
3. Heat the remaining oil, then fry the ginger, garlic and chilli for about 2 minutes until golden. Remove from the heat and add the spring onions. Splash the fish with a little soy sauce and spoon the contents of the pan over the top.

Creamy sprout and leek colcannon with pan-fried calf's liver

Serves 2

Potatoes are a good source of magnesium. Brussels sprouts are very high in sulphoraphane and are protective against many cancers. Liver is high in bio-available iron and essential B vitamins.

- 2 large floury potatoes (e.g. baking potatoes), peeled and chopped into 1 cm/½ in cubes
- 2 tbsp olive oil
- 1 leek, thinly sliced
- 6 Brussels sprouts, thinly sliced
- 25 g/1 oz of butter
- 4 tbsp milk
- salt and freshly ground black pepper
- 2 pieces organic calf's liver, thinly sliced

1. Put the potatoes in a saucepan of cold water and bring to the boil. Cook for 15 minutes, or until the tender.
2. Put the oil in a frying pan and add the sliced leek and Brussels sprouts. Stir to coat the vegetables with the oil, then cover the pan with a lid on and cook over a gentle heat for 10 minutes, stirring occasionally.
3. When the vegetables are tender mash them together with the butter and milk, then season with the salt and pepper, to taste.
4. Heat a splash of olive oil in a frying pan and when really hot, add the calf's liver and sauté for 2 minutes each side. Season with salt and pepper, then serve on top of the colcannon.

Treats

Spiced Earl Grey tea loaf

Serves 6

This is a delicious teatime treat, and the fibre and phytonutrients will be fuelling your cells and working to support your gut health. Citrus zest contains D-limonene, which belongs to the family of terpenes. Terpenes are aromatic oils and usually smell good. They also provide support for the detoxification of oestrogens and have anti-inflammatory properties as well. The tea contains polyphenols such as theaflavins, tannins and flavonoids, which act as antioxidants for quenching scavenging free radicals.

- coconut oil, for greasing
- 2 tea bags
- 60 g/2¼ oz dark brown muscovado sugar
- 250 g/9 oz mixed dried fruit
- 275 g/9¾ oz plain wholemeal flour/all-purpose wholewheat flour
- 2½ tsp baking powder
- 1 tsp ground mixed spice
- ½ tsp cinnamon
- ¼ tsp salt
- zest of 1 large orange
- 2 large free-range eggs, beaten

1. Preheat the oven to 200°C/180°C fan/gas mark 6, and grease and line a 900 g/2 lb loaf tin.
2. Boil 300 ml/10½ fl oz/1¼ cups + 1 tbsp water and pour into a jug containing the tea bags. After a few minutes, discard the bags.
3. Add the sugar and dried fruit to the tea in the jug.
4. Put the flour, baking powder, mixed spice, cinnamon, salt and grated orange zest in a separate bowl. Pour the contents of the jug over the dry ingredients, stir well, then stir in the egg as well.
5. Pour the mixture into the prepared loaf tin, smooth the top, and bake for 1 hour or until firm, risen and golden and leave to cool.

Drinks

Mexican chilli hot chocolate

Serves 1

Arriba arriba! Bring on the dark chocolate! This is a proanthocyanidin that may stimulate gene expression and immune response. It is a delicious anti-inflammatory and contains magnesium, which is required in Phase 1 and Phase 2 detoxification.

- 25 g/1 oz dark chocolate
- 1 tbsp unsweetened cocoa powder
- pinch of chilli flakes
- 250 ml/9 fl oz/1 cup + 2 tbsp milk
- maple syrup (optional)

1. Put all the ingredients in a small saucepan and heat but don't allow the mixture to boil. Strain the hot chocolate into a mug and sweeten with maple syrup (if using), to taste.

Mo-tea-to mocktail

Serves 2

Numerous studies have shown green tea to be an effective antioxidant and protective against chronic diseases. Green tea contains the catechin EGCG (epigallocatechin gallate), an antioxidant compound. Make use of this recipe for oxidative stress and inflammation, too.

Mint is not just for decoration. Mint was originally used as a medicinal herb to treat stomach ache. It contains rosmarinic acid and gets its aroma from menthol. Mint has also been used for centuries to help alleviate symptoms of hay fever and the common cold.

- 2 green tea bags
- 250 ml/9 fl oz/1 cup + 2 tbsp boiling water
- 2 limes, quartered
- 2 tsp demerara sugar
- handful of mint
- ice

1. Put the tea bags in a jug of boiling water and infuse for 5 minutes. Remove the bags and put the jug in the fridge until chilled.
2. When ready to serve, put the lime quarters in a jug and add the sugar and mint. Crush the lime and the mint with the end of a rolling pin or pestle to release the juice from the lime and the oil from the mint. Add the tea and the ice and mix everything together, then strain and pour into a cocktail glass.

Green smoothie

Serves 1

A delicious green smoothie that doesn't taste of lawn cuttings! Spinach supports detoxification due to its high folate content and it is also an excellent source of vitamin K, vitamin A, vitamin C, vitamin B2, manganese, magnesium and iron.

- 125 ml/4 fl oz/½ cup plain, live yogurt
- handful of spinach leaves
- 2 tsp pure honey
- ½ banana (pre-sliced and frozen)
- juice of 1 lime
- ½ tsp vanilla essence
- 50 ml/1½ fl oz/3 tbsp milk (or milk substitute)

1. Put all the ingredients in a blender and purée until smooth. Add more milk if too thick.

Chapter 5

Methylation

Folate is an important vitamin belonging to the B Complex group of vitamins and ensuring we have adequate amounts in our daily diet is essential. Folate, vitamin B6 and vitamin B12 are important for the synthesis of DNA, and for maintaining a balance in the methylation pathways. Due to our genetic predisposition (as well as gut function) we may differ in the way we absorb and metabolize B vitamins.

What is methylation?
Methylation is the process whereby our DNA is repaired and new DNA produced. As well as DNA repair and replication, methylation directs folate from our diet to be remethylated (recycled) into homocysteine.

Homocysteine is an amino acid (building blocks of proteins) produced during the methylation cycle. Homocysteine needs to be further metabolized to methionine with the help of vitamin B12 and folate. This process has widespread implications for health-related conditions. High levels of homocysteine are a risk factor linked to cardiovascular disease, some forms of cancer and neurological disorders and particularly, Alzheimer's Disease.

Methylation is a complex process that takes place constantly in almost all our cells, year after year, using folate (B9) and vitamin B6 and B12 to complete this ongoing cycle. Think of methylation as a system of gears and switches where each turn of the gears affects the way the next switch works. If there is insufficient energy to drive this system, a build-up of one chemical or a lack of another causes the machinery to slow down, grind to a halt or sometimes speed up.

Vitamin B12 plays a vital role in DNA repair and energy production. B12 is one of the important micronutrients in the human diet and a lack of

B12 leads to neurological conditions, anaemia, and altered homocysteine metabolism. B12 is considered a nootropic (substances that can boost brain performance) because it may enhance cognitive function, improve motivation, focus and concentration. Deficiency in vitamin B12 has been linked to depression, bipolar disorder, dementia and stroke. Most animal protein contains B12, but vegan diets often lack this vital nutrient. Spirulina and nori may be viable sources for vegans, however, supplementation may be required for some people.

Why is methylation important?
Scientific knowledge can help us understand that individual requirements for certain ingredients and vitamins vary between populations and certainly between individuals. The nutrients in the common foods found in this chapter play a vital role, acting as chemical messengers within our cells. Eating to support methylation pathways is a great way to increase energy levels and improve all-round health.

The interactions and delicate balance between the *folate*, *methionine* and *trans-sulphuration pathways* play vital roles in mental and neurological illnesses and a wide range of chronic and age-related diseases.

When we are stressed or feeling 'low', it's often a result of the methylation cycle working very hard and using more B vitamins than usual. This is why vitamin B is often recommended for stress and mental fatigue.

DNA methylation is a critical epigenetic process. Epigenetics is the effect that our environment has on our genes. In the brain this is called 'neuroepigenetics'. This is the notion that our genes as well as our environment can alter brain function.

Brain development is a constant process of neurogenesis (building up) and neurodegeneration (breaking down) of cells throughout our lifetimes. Emerging studies are showing the links between disruption in the methylation pathways with delayed brain development and psychiatric illnesses.

Methylation affects biochemical reactions in our body that are essential for:

- *Cardiovascular* (heart and vessel) *health*
- *Neurotransmitter production* (moods and disorders)
- *Detoxification* (internal cleaning)
- *Oestrogen function* (sex hormones)
- *Male and female reproductive function* (pregnancy and male fertility)
- *Fat metabolism* and *energy production*

Eat more folate

At some point in our lives, most of us have been told 'Eat your greens' because leafy greens like spinach, kale and lettuce are good for us. Have you ever wondered why?

Popeye was spot on! Leafy greens contain folate, which is one of the B vitamins we need for optimal health.

Disruptions in folate metabolism are common causes of certain cancers, neurological disorders and developmental issues in the foetus such as neural tube defects (spina bifida, cleft palate and miscarriage). This is the reason why pregnant women are advised to supplement with folic acid during pregnancy.

Abnormal folate metabolism affects all processes of methylation, such as DNA repair and DNA replication. Our DNA is copied over and over again as cells divide throughout our lifetimes. As we age, this process becomes slower and less efficient, and until the scientists have revealed the cure for ageing, we will have to do our best to maintain our health with nutrients, brain stimulation and physical exercise.

Individuals suffering from Crohn's disease, celiac disease or inflammatory bowel issues may need to supplement with folic acid or a methylated form of folate called methylfolate, due to malabsorption issues in the gut. Clinical data suggests that people with low folic acid levels and high homocysteine levels are at an increased risk for Alzheimer's disease. Impaired methylation results in oxidative DNA damage and increases the risk for neurodegenerative disease.

Additional support can be provided by enhancing the detoxification pathway. This requires eating cruciferous vegetables as well as avoiding excessive exposure to toxins. Many of the cruciferous (cabbage, broccoli, cauliflower, Brussels sprouts) and allium (onions, garlic) vegetables that we mentioned in Chapter 4 are also called 'sulphurous foods'. Sulphur is a key component for the end-product of methylation, which produces glutathione.

Foods high in folate are spinach, kale, lettuce, rocket, watercress, asparagus, broccoli, parsley, avocado, celery, oranges.

Vitamin B12

Vitamin B12 is another important nutrient that is needed for optimal methylation. If you are vegan, be sure to keep a check on your vitamin B12 status as B12 is found primarily in animal products. Shitake mushrooms and nori contain sources of vitamin B12 for vegan diets.

If you test low for B12 and have a low dietary intake of B12-rich foods, it would be advisable to supplement with vitamin B12.

A lack of B12 leads to demyelination. The myelin sheath is a fatty covering that protects nerve cells in the brain and can be compared to insulation tape on electrical wires. Demyelination causes scar tissue to form on the myelin, so nerves cannot transmit brain signals effectively, and the instructions from the brain are blocked or faulty. A disruption in nerve signalling can be permanent or transient depending on the extent of the scarring or damage. There are, of course, other causes of demyelination and diseases such as multiple sclerosis, inflammatory autoimmune disorders, and some viral infections are a result of complex demyelination.

Eggs are a good source of vitamin B12 and choline, which is another important nutrient in methylation.

Choline

Choline is often overlooked but is important in the methylation pathway. Choline performs vital functions ranging from cell structure to neurotransmitter synthesis, and choline deficiency is now considered to impact liver disease, atherosclerosis and possibly neurological disorders such as schizophrenia and autism. Choline together with vitamin B6, B12, and folate help complete the methylation cycle which recycles molecules and keeps donating them to other groups of compounds so that they in turn can do their biochemical job effectively. If there is a backup in the pathway or insufficient supply of these donated molecules, more toxic compounds are formed in higher amounts. One of them being homocysteine. A build-up of homocysteine that is not efficiently methylated shows up on blood tests and will raise your medical practitioner's eyebrows. High homocysteine levels are linked to cardiovascular disease, cancer, cognitive decline (brain ageing) and bone fractures.

Recent studies show that choline supplementation during critical periods of neonatal development can have long-term benefits for memory. Pregnant women should be advised to supplement with choline and folic acid during their pregnancy.

Sources of choline are eggs (must include the yolk!), chicken liver, chicken and salmon. *Vegan sources* (although not nearly as high as animal sources) are soya/soy flour, quinoa, cauliflower, peas and almonds.

Your Healing Kitchen

Ingredients known to support methylation include: spinach, kale (not raw), parsley, celery, lettuce, dark leafy greens, avocado, broccoli, peas, asparagus, cauliflower, oranges, eggs, milk, cheese, yogurt, chicken, fish, red meat, chickpeas, whey protein powder, Marmite®.

Fast food

- Freshly squeezed orange juice
- Greek yogurt with seeds, fresh fruit and fresh mint
- Spinach omelette
- Grilled chicken
- Green salad with lettuce, fresh parsley, raw broccoli florets and celery
- Pot of edamame beans
- Whey protein shake
- Grilled chicken and rocket sandwich

Easy recipes

BREAKFAST

Orange and date fruit salad
Superberry smoothie
Middle Eastern breakfast bowl

MAIN MEALS

Easy watercress and spinach soup
Pearl barley, feta, parsley and cashew nut salad
Broccoli and sweet potato curried fritters
Star anise slow-cooked beef ribs
(served with Sesame spinach)
Japanese baked salmon with
brown rice and edamame
Shakshuka

SNACKS

Pea and mint dip
Baked beetroot crisps
Kale crisps

DRINKS

Mango and orange lassi
Celery, apple, mint
and kiwi summer smoothie

Breakfast

Orange and date fruit salad

Serves 4

Oranges are not only a source of vitamin C; they contain folate and beta-carotene as well.

- 6 oranges, peeled and finely sliced
- 4 pitted Medjool dates, chopped
- 1 tbsp honey
- 1 tbsp lemon juice
- 1 tsp cinnamon
- 50 g/1¾ oz slivered almonds

1. Place the oranges and dates in a bowl. Add the honey. lemon juice and cinnamon and toss to coat the fruit. Stir in the almonds. Cover and refrigerate, and serve chilled.

Superberry smoothie

Serves 1

The antioxidant benefits of red and blue berries are widespread and support methylation, reduction in oxidative stress, reduction in inflammation and detoxification. Almond milk is high in vitamin E and calcium and is an ideal substitute for people following plant-based diets or who are lactose intolerant.

- 150 g/5½ oz mixture of cherries, strawberries and blueberries (either fresh or frozen)
- 100 ml/3½ fl oz/7 tbsp almond milk
- 1 large date (for sweetness)

1. Put all the ingredients in a blender and blitz.

Middle Eastern breakfast bowl

Serves 2

Tahini seems to have originated in ancient Persia and is made from ground, roasted sesame seeds. These tiny seeds are packed with nutrients such as copper, zinc, iron, selenium, and a high percentage of magnesium. Magnesium is a vital nutrient in the methylation pathways and is needed for more than 200 biological processes in the body. Folate found in baby spinach leaves has far-reaching effects for methylation, originating in the folate cycle.

- 4 tbsp 5% Greek yogurt
- 2 spring onions/scallions
- 2 medium tomatoes, chopped
- handful of baby spinach leaves
- ½ red pepper/red bell pepper, diced
- ½ cucumber, diced
- 1 tbsp tahini
- juice of ½ lemon
- 1 small red chilli (optional)
- drizzle of olive oil
- salt and freshly ground black pepper

1. Divide all of the ingredients between two bowls. Season with salt and pepper, to taste, and enjoy!

Main meals

Easy watercress and spinach soup

Serves 2

This is the ultimate quick-fix of leafy greens when you don't fancy a salad.

- 100 g/3.5 oz spinach
- 100 g/3.5 oz watercress
- 2 spring onions/scallions, sliced
- 200 ml/7 fl oz/¾ cup + 2 tbsp vegetable or chicken stock
- 1 medium-sized, ripe avocado
- 75 g/2½ oz cooked rice (white or brown)
- juice of ½ lemon
- 2 tbsp mixed seeds, plus extra to serve
- salt and freshly ground black pepper

1. Put all the ingredients in a blender and whizz until smooth. Heat in a large saucepan until piping hot. Season with salt and pepper, to taste.
2. Serve with some toasted seeds scattered on top if you want added crunch.

Pearl barley, feta, parsley and cashew nut salad

Serves 4

Pearl barley is an ideal source of fibre and contains magnesium. Barley is high in vitamin C and folate, an essential element for enhancing methylation pathways.

- 80 g/2¾ oz pearl barley
- 150 g/5½ oz feta, crumbled
- large packet of flat leaf parsley, roughly chopped
- 4 spring onions/scallions
- 1 green pepper/green bell pepper, chopped into little cubes
- 40 g/1½ oz cashew nuts, lightly toasted
- 1 tsp coriander/cilantro seeds, lightly toasted and bashed
- ½ tsp ground cumin
- 4 tbsp olive oil
- 2 garlic cloves, peeled and crushed
- 2 tbsp lemon juice
- salt and freshly ground black pepper

1. Put the barley in a saucepan and cover with a generous amount of cold water. Bring to a slow boil and cook for about 20 minutes, taking care not to let all of the water evaporate.
2. Drain the barley and put it in a bowl with the feta, parsley, spring onions, green pepper, cashew nuts, coriander seeds and cumin.
3. Finally, mix the olive oil with the garlic and lemon juice and dress the salad. Season with salt and pepper, to taste.

Broccoli and sweet potato curried fritters

Serves 2

Broccoli contains multiple vitamins and antioxidants needed for optimal methylation, detoxification and oxidative stress. Folic acid, sulphoraphane, fibre, vitamin C and vitamin K are packed into these little green powerhouses.

- 1 large broccoli floret, very finely chopped
- 1 medium red pepper/red bell pepper finely chopped
- 300 g/10½ oz sweet potato, peeled and grated
- 2 spring onions/scallions, thinly sliced
- salt and freshly ground black pepper
- 2 tbsp curry powder
- 40 g/1½ oz plain flour/all-purpose flour
- 120 ml/4 fl oz/½ cup milk
- 2 eggs, lightly beaten
- 2 tbsp rapeseed/canola oil

To serve
- 150 g/5½ oz plain low-fat Greek yogurt
- 2 tbsp mango chutney

1. Combine the broccoli, red pepper, sweet potato and spring onions in a bowl. Season with salt and pepper.
2. Add the curry powder, flour, milk and eggs. Mix well.
3. Heat the oil in a large frying pan over a medium-high heat.
   Place 1 tbsp batter at a time in the pan, making sure the fritters are not too close together and adding extra oil if needed. Fry the fritters for 3–4 minutes on each side, or until well browned.
4. Transfer the cooked fritters to a plate lined with a paper towel and cover them loosely with another paper towel to keep warm.
5. Combine the yogurt and mango chutney in a bowl and serve with the fritters.

Star anise slow-cooked beef ribs

Serves 4

Vitamin B12 plays a central role in reducing an overload of homocysteine. High homocysteine is associated with dementia, Alzheimer's disease, and cardiovascular disease. Beef contains significant amounts of vitamin B12, vitamin B6, choline, niacin, iron, zinc and selenium.

- 1 tbsp olive oil
- 1 kg/2 lb 4 oz beef short ribs (approximately 4 large ribs)
- 1 large onion, peeled and chopped
- 2 garlic cloves, peeled and crushed
- 20 g/¾ oz ginger root, peeled and grated
- 2 star anise
- 3 tbsp dark soy sauce
- 500 ml/17 fl oz/2 cups fresh beef or chicken stock
- salt and freshly ground black pepper
- juice of 1 lime

1. Heat the oil in a large casserole dish with an ovenproof lid. Season the short ribs and brown over a medium-high heat for 3–4 minutes on all sides (you may need to do this in batches, adding a little more oil), then remove with a slotted spoon.
2. Add the onion to the casserole dish and fry for 5 minutes, until golden and starting to soften, then add the garlic and ginger and cook for a further 2 minutes. Add the star anise, soy sauce and stock. Return the meat to the pan with any resting juices, bring to the boil, then reduce to a simmer.
3. Put a lid on the pan and put in the oven at 180°C/160°C fan/gas mark 4 for 3 hours, until the meat is very tender. Season with salt and pepper and add lime juice, to taste.
4. Serve with Sesame spinach (see below).

Sesame spinach

Serves 4

Spinach supports detoxification thanks to its high folate content. It is also an excellent source of vitamin K, vitamin A, vitamin C, vitamin B2, manganese, magnesium and iron.

- 450 g/14 oz spinach
- 2 tbsp sesame oil
- 1 garlic clove, crushed
- 2 tbsp sesame seeds
- 2 tbsp soy sauce
- 3 spring onions/scallions, finely sliced

1. Put the spinach in a saucepan and wilt for 1 minute on a high heat. Remove the spinach and heat the oil, frying the crushed garlic for 1 minute. Add the spinach and all the other ingredients to the pan, stir to combine and turn off the heat.
2. Serve with Star anise slow-cooked beef ribs (see above).

Japanese baked salmon with brown rice and edamame

Serves 2

Salmon is high in omega-3 fatty acids, protein and the antioxidant astaxanthin. Brown rice is a good source of fibre and manganese and is gluten free. Edamame support oestrogen and contain high amounts of folate.

- 2 salmon fillets (about 130 g/4¾ oz each), skin on and boneless

Marinade
- 1 tsp sesame oil
- 1 tbsp soy sauce
- 1 spring onion/scallions, sliced
- 1 garlic clove, crushed

Brown rice and edamame
- 250 g/9 oz brown rice
- 175 g/6 oz frozen soya beans/edamame
- 1 tbsp soy sauce
- 1 tbsp extra virgin olive oil
- 2 tsp ginger, finely grated
- 1 garlic clove, crushed

To serve
- 4 spring onions/scallions, thinly sliced

1. Preheat the oven to 200°C/180°C fan/gas mark 6.
2. Place the salmon fillets skin side down on a large rectangle of kitchen foil inside a small baking dish, so that they fit snugly. Mix together the sesame oil, soy sauce, spring onion and garlic for the marinade and pour over the fish. Scrunch the silver foil (or use parchment paper) to form a loose parcel around the fish and the marinade so it cooks in its own steam. Bake for 12 minutes then remove from the oven and keep warm.
3. Meanwhile, make the brown rice and edamame. Cook the rice following the pack instructions, adding the edamame during the final 2 minutes of cooking.
4. Mix together the soy sauce, olive oil, ginger and garlic. Drain the cooked rice and edamame, transfer to a serving bowl and stir in the soy sauce mixture. Scatter with the spring onions and serve alongside the salmon.

Shakshuka

Serves 2

Eggs are an ideal source of choline, protein, vitamin B6, vitamin B12 and vitamin D. Vegetables support an anti-inflammatory diet.

- 1 tbsp olive oil
- 1 small onion, peeled and sliced
- 1 red pepper/red bell pepper, cut into long slices
- 1 green pepper/green bell pepper, cut into long slices
- salt and freshly ground black pepper
- 1 garlic clove, finely chopped
- ½ tsp cumin seeds
- ½ tsp caraway seeds
- ¼ tsp cayenne
- 1 tbsp tomato purée
- 1 400 g/14 oz box or bottle tomatoes
- 1 tsp sugar (optional)
- small bunch of coriander/cilantro, roughly chopped
- small bunch of parsley, roughly chopped
- 4 eggs

1. Heat the oil in a large frying pan. Add the onion and peppers and season with salt and pepper. Cook over a medium heat for 3–4 minutes until softened. Add the garlic and cook for a further 2 minutes, then sprinkle the cumin, caraway seeds and cayenne into the pan. Stir in the tomato purée and tomatoes.
2. Simmer the sauce for about 10 minutes, uncovered, until it has reduced a little.
3. Taste after 5 minutes and add a little sugar if you think the tomatoes need it. Keep an eye on the texture – you don't want the sauce runny, but it mustn't be too dry either. If it looks dry, add a splash of water.
4. When the sauce is reduced, stir in the herbs.
5. Make 4 little wells in the sauce. One at a time, break the eggs into a cup and drop them carefully into the wells. Cook for a few more minutes until the whites are just set and the yolks are still runny.
6. Serve with extra coriander sprinkled on top.

Tip: You could make double quantities of the tomato sauce to serve over pasta.

Snacks

Pea and mint dip

Serves 4

Peas are high in folate and magnesium, potassium, calcium and fibre – so much goodness in something so little!

- 500 g/1 lb 2 oz frozen peas
- small bunch of fresh mint leaves
- 1 garlic clove, crushed
- 2 tbsp tahini
- 4 tbsp lemon juice
- 2 tbsp olive oil
- pinch of salt

1. Cook the peas in boiling water for 3 minutes, then allow to cool.
2. Put all the ingredients in a blender and blitz until smooth.
3. Serve with seeded bread or with any 'dippable' veggies.

Baked beetroot crisps

Serves 2

Beetroot/beet contains betaine, which is required in the methylation pathway.

- 250 g/9 oz fresh uncooked beetroot/beet
- 4 tbsp of olive oil
- pinch of salt

1. Preheat the oven to 220°C/200°C fan/gas mark 7.
2. Using a mandoline, slice the beetroot into very fine disks. Toss in the olive oil and salt.
3. Spread the beetroot on large baking tray and roast for about 25 minutes until crisp. Allow to cool.
4. Serve with hummus.

Kale crisps

Serves 4

Kale provides folate, vitamin K, lots of fibre and vitamin C.

- 200 g/7 oz kale, thick stems removed
- 2 tbsp olive oil
- good pinch of salt
- small pinch chilli flakes (optional)

1. Preheat the oven to 220°C/200°C fan/gas mark 6.
2. Put the kale on a baking tray and pour the oil over it. Using your hands, mix the kale with the oil and sprinkle with the salt and chilli (if using).
3. Bake the kale in the oven for 10 minutes. Keep an eye on the crisps while they cook, and from time to time stir the kale with a spoon so it can brown at the edges and crisp up. It will shrink a little during cooking and be slightly charred.
4. Serve the crisps as soon as they are cool enough to eat.

Drinks

Mango and orange lassi

Serves 2

Surprisingly, oranges contain folate, even though they are not green. This is great news if you need to increase folate intake in picky eaters who are not partial to green stuff! Mangoes also contain folate. In addition, mangoes are a good source of antioxidants, are beneficial for eye health, assist with constipation and help to improve gut microflora.

- 1 large mango, peeled and cut into chunks
- 1 large orange, skinned and halved
- 125 ml/4 fl oz/½ cup plain Greek yogurt
- 125 ml/4 fl oz/½ cup milk
- 1 tbsp honey
- 1 cup ice cubes

1. Put all the ingredients in a blender and blitz until smooth and creamy.

Celery, apple, mint and kiwi summer smoothie

Serves 1

The combined fibre, folate and vitamins make this a super smoothie. It is great for those who are stressed out or run down and is ideal to drink on the go.

- 1 celery stick
- 1 apple, peeled and sliced
- handful of fresh mint
- 2 fresh ripe kiwi, skin removed
- handful of ice cubes

1. Put all the ingredients in a blender and blitz until smooth.

References and Further Reading

Introduction

1. Simopoulos, A.P. (2010) Nutrigenetics/nutrigenomics. *Annual Review of Public Health 31*, 53–68.

2. Watson, J.D. & Crick, F.H.C. (1953) Molecular structure of nucleic acids: A structure for deoxyribose nucleic acid. *Nature 171*, 737–738.

3. Liu, R.H. (2003) Health benefits of fruit and vegetables are from additive and synergistic combinations of phytochemicals. *American Journal of Clinical Nutrition 78*(3 Suppl), 517S–520S.

4. Doleman, J.F., Grisar, K., Van Liedekerke, L., Saha, S. *et al.* (2017) The contribution of alliaceous and cruciferous vegetables to dietary sulphur intakes. *Food Chemistry 234*, 38–45.

5. Milner, J.A. (2008) Nutrition and cancer: Essential elements for the roadmap. *Cancer Letters 269*(2), 189–198.

6. Ferguson, J.F., Phillips, C.M., McMonagle, J., Pérez-Martinez, P. *et al* (2010) NOS3 gene polymorphisms are associated with risk markers of cardiovascular disease and interact with omega-3 polyunsaturated fatty acids. *Atherosclerosis 211*(2), 539–544.

7. Schulz. L.C. (2010) The Dutch Hunger Winter and the developmental origins of health and disease. *PNAS 107*(39), 16757–16758.

Chapter 1 – Genes at Work

1. Zardast, M., Namakin, K., Kaho, J.A, & Hashemi, S.S. (2016) Assessment of antibacterial effect of garlic on patients infected with *Helicobacter pylori* using urease breath test. *Avicenna Journal of Phytomedicine 5*(5), 495–501.

2. Bailey, D.T., Dalton, C., Joseph Daugherty, F. & Tempesta, M.S. (2007) Can a concentrated cranberry extract prevent recurring urinary tract infections in women? *Phytomedicine 14*(4), 237–241.

3. Yang L., Palliyaguru, D.L. & Kensler, D.W. (2016) Frugal chemoprotective targeting Nrf2 with foods rich in sulforaphane. *Seminars in Oncology 43*(1), 146–153.

4. Lewis, K.N., Mele, J., Hayes, J.D. & Buffenstein, R. (2010) Nrf2, a guardian of healthspan and gatekeeper of species longevity. *Integrative and Comparative Biology 50*(5), 829–843.

5. Russo, M., Spagnuolo, C., Tedesco, I. & Russo, G.L. (2010) Phytochemicals in cancer prevention and therapy: Truth or dare? *Toxins 2*(4), 517–551.

6. Liu, R.H. (2003) Health benefits of fruit and vegetables are from additive and synergistic combinations of phytochemicals. *American Journal of Clinical Nutrition 78*(3 Suppl) 517S–520S.

7. Lui, R.H. (2013) Dietary bioactive compounds and their health implications. *Journal of Food Science 78*(Suppl 1), A18–A25.

8. Gammone, M.A., Riccioni, G. & D'Orazio, N. (2015) Carotenoids: Potential allies of cardiovascular health? *Food & Nutrition Research 59*(1), 26762.

Chapter 2 – Inflammation

1. Minehane, A.M., Vinoy, S., Russell, W.R., Baka, A. *et al.* (2015) Low-grade inflammation, diet composition and health: Current research evidence and its translation. *British Journal of Nutrition 114*(7), 999–1012.

2. Panicker, K.S. & Jewell, D.E. (2015) The beneficial role of anti-inflammatory dietary ingredients in attenuating markers of low-grade inflammation in aging. *Hormone Molecular Biology and Clinical Investigation 23*(2), 58–70.

3. Calder, P.C., Ahluwalia, N., Albers, R., Bosco, N. *et al.* (2013) A consideration of biomarkers to be used for evaluation of inflammation in human nutritional studies. *British Journal of Nutrition 108*(Suppl 1), S1–S34.

4. Devaraj, S., Hemarajata, P. & Versalovic, J. (2013) The human gut microbiome and body metabolism: Implications for obesity and diabetes. *Clinical Chemistry 59*(4), 617–628.

5. Ganel, S.C. *et al.*, Sanos, S.L., Kalfass, C., Oberle, K. *et al.* (2012) Priming of natural killer cells by non-mucosal mononuclear phagocytes requires instructive signals from commensal microbiota. *Immunity 37*(1), 171–186.

6. Carvalho, B.M. & Saad, M.J.A. (2013) Influence of gut microbiota on subclinical inflammation and insulin resistance. *Mediators of Inflammation.* DOI: 10.1155/2013/986734

7. Miller, A.H., Maletic, V. & Raison, A.L. (2009) Inflammation and its discontents: The role of cytokines in the pathophysiology of major depression. *Biological Psychiatry 65*(9), 732–741.

8. Bischoff, S.C., Barbara, G., Buurman, W., Ockhuizen, T. *et al.* (2014) Intestinal permeability – a new target for disease prevention and therapy. *BMC Gastroenterology 14*, 189.

9. Cho, I. & Blaser, M.J. (2012) The human microbiome: At the interface of health and disease. *Nature Reviews. Genetics 13*(4), 260–270.

10. Durchschein, F. *et al.*, Petritsch, W. & Hammer, H.F. (2016) Diet therapy for inflammatory bowel disease: The established and the new. *World Journal of Gastroenterology 22*(7), 2179–2194.

11. Panossian, A. (2003) Adaptogens: Tonic herbs for fatigue and stress. *Alternative and Complementary Therapies 9*(6). DOI: 10.1089/107628003322658610

12. Cohen, S., Janicki-Deverts, D., Doyle, W.J., Miller, G.E. *et al.* (2012) Chronic stress, glucocorticoid receptor resistance, inflammation and disease risk. *Proceedings of the National Academy of Sciences of the USA 109*(16), 5995–5999.

13. Costedio, M.M., Hyman, N. & Mawe, G.M. (2007) Serotonin and its role in colonic function and in gastrointestinal disorders. *Diseases of the Colon and Rectum 50*(3), 376–388.

14. Yarnell, E. & Abascal, K. (2006) Herbs for curbing inflammation. *Alternative and Complementary Therapies 12*(1). DOI: 10.1089/act.2006.12.22

15. Borelli, F. & Izzo, A.A. (2000) The plant kingdom as a source of anti-ulcer remedies. *Phytotherapy Research 14*(8), 581–591.

16. Kromhout, D., Geleijnse, J.M. & Shimokawa, H. (2012) Fish oil and omega-3 fatty acids in cardiovascular disease: Do they really work? *European Heart Journal 33*(4), 436–443.

17. Engler, M., Chen, C.Y., Malloy, M.J., Browne, A. *et al.* (2004) Flavonoid-rich dark chocolate improves endothelial function and increases plasma epicatechin concentrations in healthy adults. *Journal of the American College of Nutrition 23*(3), 197–204.

18. Katz, D.L., Doughty, K. & Ali, A. (2013) Cocoa and chocolate in human health and disease. *Antioxidants and Redox Signaling 15*(10), 2779–2811.

19. Arranz, S., Valderas-Martinez, P., Chiva-Blanch, G., Casas, R. *et al.* (2013) Cardioprotective effects of cocoa: Clinical evidence from randomized clinical intervention trials in humans. *Molecular Nutrition and Food Research 57*(6), 936–947.

20. Ferrari, C.K. (2004) Functional foods, herbs and nutraceuticals: Towards biochemical mechanisms of healthy aging. *Biogerontology* 5(5), 275–289.

21. Miller, N. & Ruiz-Larrea, M. (2002) Flavonoids and other plant polyphenols in the diet: Their significance as antioxidants. *Journal of Nutritional and Environmental Medicine* 12(1), 39–51.

22. Zhang, J.M. & An, J. (2007) Cytokines inflammation and pain. *International Anaesthesiology Clinics* 45(2), 27–37.

23. Pahwa, R., Singh, A. & Jialal, I. (2019) *Chronic Inflammation*. StatPearls Publishing.

24. Carabotti, M., Scirocco, A., Maselli, M.A. & Severi, C. (2015) The gut-brain axis: Interactions between enteric microbiota, central and enteric nervous systems. *Annals of Gastroenterology* 28(2), 203–209.

25. Foster, J.A., Lyte, M., Meyer, E. & Cryan, J.F. (2016) Gut microbiota and brain function: An evolving field in neuroscience. *International Journal of Neuropsychopharmacology* 19(5).

26. Rani, A.R., Ali, R.A.R. & Lee, Y.Y. (2016) Irritable bowel syndrome and inflammatory bowel disease overlap syndrome: Pieces of the puzzle falling into place. *Intestinal Research* 14(4), 297–304.

27. Jung, U.J. & Choi, M.S. (2014) Obesity and its metabolic complications: The role of adipokines and the relationship between obesity, inflammation, and dyslipidemia. *International Journal of Molecular Sciences* 15(4), 6184–6223.

Chapter 3 – Oxidative Stress

1. Pham-Huy, L.A., He, H. & Pham-Huy, C. (2008) Free radicals in disease and health. *International Journal of Biomedical Science* 4(2), 89–96.

2. Uttara, B., Singh, A.V., Zamboni, P. & Mahajan, R.T. (2009) Oxidative stress and neurodegenerative disease: A review of upstream and downstream antioxidant therapeutic options. *Current Neuropharmacology* 7(1), 65–74.

3. Thomson, C.D., Chisholm, A., McLachlan, S.K. & Campbell, J.M. (2008) Brazil nuts: An effective way to improve selenium status. *American Journal of Clinical Nutrition* 87(2), 379–384.

4. Salim, S. (2014) Oxidative stress and psychological disorders. *Current Neuropharmacology* 12(2), 140–147.

5. Hirsch, E.C. (1994) Biochemistry of Parkinson's disease with special reference to the dopaminergic systems. *Molecular Neurobiology* 9(1–3), 135–142.

6. Bredesen, D.E., Amos, C.E., Canick, J., Ackerley, M. *et al.* (2016) Reversal of cognitive decline in Alzheimer's disease. *Impact of Aging (Albany NY) 8*(5), 1250–1258.

7. Ceriello, A. & Motz, E. (2004) Insulin resistance: Is oxidative stress the pathogenic mechanism underlying insulin resistance, diabetes and cardiovascular disease? The common soil hypothesis revisited. *Arteriosclerosis, Thrombosis, and Vascular Biology 24*(5), 816–823.

8. Block, G. (1992) Fruit and vegetables, and cancer prevention: A review of the epidemiological evidence. *Nutrition and Cancer: 18*(1), 1–29.

9. Le Marchand, L., Murphy, S.P., Hankin, J.H., Wilkens, L.R. & Kolonel, L.N. (2009) Intake of flavonoids and lung cancer. *Journal of the National Cancer Institute 82*(2), 154–160.

10. Boyle, S.P., Dobson, V.L., Duthie, S.J., Kyle, J.A. & Collins, A.R. (2000) Absorption and DNA protective effects of flavonoid glycosides from an onion meal. *European Journal of Nutrition 39*(5), 213–223.

11. Knekt, P., Jarvinen, R., Reunanen, A. & Maatela, J. (1996) Flavonoid intake and coronary mortality in Finland: A cohort study. *British Medical Journal 312*(7029), 478–481.

12. Brosnan, J.T. & Brosnan, M.E. (2006) The sulfur-containing amino acids: An overview. *Journal of Nutrition 136*(6 Suppl), 1636S–1640S.

13. Liu, R.H. (2003) Health benefits of fruit and vegetables are from additive and synergistic combinations of phytochemicals. *American Journal of Clinical Nutrition 78*(3 Suppl) 517S–520S.

14. Sies, H. (2015) Oxidative stress: A concept in redox biology and medicine. Redox Biology. *Elsevier B.V. 4*, 180–183.

15. Caio, E.G.R., Ribero, D.N. & Costa, N.M.B. (2012) Acute and second-meal effects of peanuts on glycaemic response and appetite in obese women with a high type 2 diabetes risk: A cross-over clinical trial. *British journal of Nutrition 109*(11),2015–2023.

Chapter 4 – Detoxification

1. Nesbert, D.W. & Vasilious, V. (2004) Analysis of the glutathione S-transferase (GTS) family. *Human Genomics 1*(6), 460–464.

2. Boddupalli, S., Mein, J.R., Lakkanna, S. & James, D.R. (2012) Induction of Phase 2 antioxidant enzymes by broccoli sulphoraphane: Perspectives in maintaining antioxidant activity of vitamins A, C and E. *Frontiers in Genetics 3*(7). DOI: 10.3389/fgene.2012.00007

3. Dinkova-Kostova, A.T., Fahey, J.W., Kostov, R.V. & Kensler, T.W (2017) KEAP1 and done? Targeting the NRF2 pathway with sulphoraphane. *Trends in Food Science and Technology 69*(Pt B), 257–269.

4. James, D., Devaraj, S., Bellur, P., Lakkanna, S., Vicini, J. & Boddupalli, S. (2012) Novel concepts of broccoli sulphoraphane and disease: Induction of Phase 2 antioxidant and detoxification enzymes by enhanced glucoraphanin in broccoli. *Nutritional Reviews 70*(11), 654–665.

5. Senger, D.R, Li, D., Jaminet, S.C. & Cao, S. (2016) Activation of the Nrf2 cell defence pathway by ancient foods: Disease prevention by important molecules and microbes lost from the modern Western diet. *PLOS One 11*(2), e0148042.

6. Van Baarden, P., Trootst, F.J., van Hemert, S., van der Meer, C. *et al.* (2009) Differential NF-Kappa pathway induction by *Lactobacillus plantarum* in the duodenum of healthy humans correlating with immune tolerance. *Proceedings of the National Academy of Sciences of the USA 106*(7), 2371–2376.

Chapter 5 – Methylation

1. Shalinske, K.L. & Shmazel, A.L. (2012) Homocysteine imbalance: A pathological metabolic marker. *Advances in Nutrition 3*(6), 755–762.

2. Nazki, F.H., Sameer, A.S. & Ganaie, B.A. (2014) Folate: Metabolism, genes, polymorphisms and associated diseases. *Gene 533*(1), 11–20.

3. Zahid, M., Beseler, C.L., Hall, J.B., LeVan, T., Cavalieri, E.L. & Rogan, E.G. (2014) Unbalanced estrogen metabolism in ovarian cancer. *International Journal of Cancer 134*(10), 2414–2423.

4. Lu, S.C. (2009) Regulation of glutathione synthesis. *Molecular Aspects of Medicine 30* (1-2), 42–59.

5. Mitchell, E.S., Conus, N. & Kaput, J.B. (2014) B vitamin polymorphisms and behaviour: Evidence of associations with neurodevelopment, depression, schizophrenia, bipolar and cognitive decline. *Neuroscience and Behavioural Reviews 47*, 307–320.

6. Zeisel, S.H. & da Costa, K.A. (2009) Choline: An essential nutrient for public health. *Nutritional Reviews 67*(11), 615–623.

7. Park, L.K., Friso, S. & Choi, S.W. (2011) Vitamins, infectious and chronic disease during adulthood and aging. Nutritional influences on epigenetics and age-related disease. *Proceedings of the Nutrition Society 71*(1), 75–83.

8. Niculescu, M.D. and Zeisel, S.H. (2002) Diet, methyl donors and DNA methylation: Interactions between dietary folate, methionine and choline. *American Society for Nutritional Sciences 132*(8 Suppl), 2333S–2335S.

A Note from Debbi and Helen

We want to say a huge thank you for choosing to read *Eat to Heal*. If you have enjoyed it and want to keep up to date with our latest releases, just sign up at the links below. Your email address will never be shared and you can unsubscribe at any time.

www.thread-books.com/debbi-nathan-and-helen-nathan

Health is a journey, not a destination. We'd be thrilled for you to join us on this journey as we attempt to demystify the science that makes us unique.

We would be really grateful if you could write a review. Maybe you have a favourite recipe from the book or one of Debbi's science explanations just 'clicks' and you want to tell the world? Don't hold back – spread the love, please!

We both regularly post information and recipes on our separate Instagrams – Debbi shares information about the latest nutrigenomic news and Helen offers free recipes and top kitchen tips. We welcome new followers. Helen also runs a cookery school if you're ever in London, and a Cook club (check out her website below for details). To book an appointment with Debbi, contact her via the Your Gene Team website.

We would love to hear from you – we wrote this book for you! So please get in touch. We promise to try and answer any questions we can – science-y or culinary.

Thanks,
Debbi and Helen

Glossary

Antioxidants – The human body produces metabolic antioxidants such as alpha lipoic acid, glutathione, L-arginine, coenzyme Q10, melatonin, uric acid, bilirubin, transferrin and metal-chelating proteins. However, we also rely heavily on obtaining antioxidants such as vitamin E, vitamin C, carotenoids, flavonoids, omega-3 and omega-6 fatty acids as well as trace minerals (zinc, selenium, manganese) from our daily food intake. To support our internal antioxidant system, we should be eating a variety of colourful antioxidants derived from plant foods or supplements.

Amino acids – Amino acids are commonly referred to as the building blocks of protein. An amino acid is an organic acid that contains carbon, hydrogen, oxygen and nitrogen. There are 20 amino acids involved in the formation of protein. The precise amount and arrangement of these amino acids is determined by the genes that encode that protein.

Amino acids are made from instructions within the genetic code, our DNA. Some amino acids function on their own and other amino acids are used as precursors (start-ups) for other molecules in the body. For example, the amino acids tryptophan, tyrosine and phenylalanine are the precursors for making the neurotransmitters serotonin, dopamine and norepinephrine.

Nine of the 20 are called essential amino acids because our bodies cannot make them and therefore we need to get them from our diet. The list includes histidine, isoleucine, leucine, lysine, valine, methionine, phenylalanine, threonine and tryptophan.

There are 11 non-essential amino acids that can be made by the human body: alanine, arginine, asparagine, aspartic acid, cysteine, glutamic acid, glutamine, glycine, proline, serine and tyrosine.

Atherosclerosis – This sometimes confusing term describes the inflammatory condition that results in the formation of plaque on the inside of the arteries that cause the arteries to narrow.

Anthocyanins – These antioxidants are a sub-category of polyphenols called flavonoids. They are usually found in red, blue, purple or even black fruits, vegetables and grains. Anthocyanins exert anti-inflammatory effects on the body and help to fight oxidative stress.

Proanthocyanidins also fall into the antioxidant sub-category of polyphenols called flavonoids. They are found in many fruits and vegetables as well as bark or rind, and they are found in certain seeds and nuts too. These powerful antioxidants have been shown to have an anti-inflammatory and anti-oxidative stress effect on human cells.

Astaxanthin – This antioxidant is part of the family of carotenoids. Astaxanthin is a red pigment and is found in a variety of seafood such as krill, wild salmon, crab, lobster and prawns. Astaxanthin can cross the blood–brain barrier and enter the brain and eye where it may influence protective anti-inflammatory and anti-oxidative stress mechanisms. Astaxanthin may also be beneficial for cardiovascular disorders, gastrointestinal and neurodegenerative disorders.

Beta-carotene – Beta-carotene is a member of the large group of antioxidants called **carotenoids**. Beta-carotene has been widely studied for its pro–vitamin A activity, meaning that beta-carotene can be converted into vitamin A once it's in the body. The most easily recognised vegetable belonging to this family is the bright orange carrot. Foods rich in the powerful antioxidant beta-carotene may be protective against heart disease and lung and mouth cancers.

Bromelain is a protein-digesting enzyme that may help with the absorption of antioxidants such as quercetin. Bromelain is found in pineapple.

Carotenoids – These antioxidants form a large family of about 500 members, with about 50 of them found in foods. However, humans can only digest and absorb about 20 of them into our tissues.

Enzymes – Enzymes are molecules (mostly proteins) that help speed up (catalyse) processes. Enzymes bind and alter compounds so that the human body can perform daily processes. Enzymes are involved in multiple biological processes from digestion to DNA replication. The enzyme lactase is found in the small intestine and is needed to break down lactose. Individuals who are lactose intolerant are not able to form the lactase enzyme.

DNA replication occurs each time a cell divides. For this to occur, the tightly coiled double-helix DNA strand needs to be unzipped by the enzyme called helicase. The two single strands of DNA are then able to replicate (copy) the DNA information using the enzyme polymerase. Enzymes are complex and vital to our survival.

Cofactors are non-protein chemicals that are needed for proteins to function. Many enzymes require cofactors to function optimally. Cofactors are 'helpers' that guide the enzyme onto the docking site of wherever they are needed. Cofactors are sometimes vitamins and sometime minerals.

Fermentation – Fermentation is the breakdown of organic substances using enzymes or micro-organisms. Micro-organisms such as yeast and bacteria produce products such as beer, wine, bread, cheese, kimchi, sauerkraut, yogurt and kefir. Fermentation is a natural process whereby the micro-organisms convert carbohydrates such as starch and sugar into alcohol or acids. The probiotics produced by naturally fermented foods are often beneficial for gut imbalances and some disorders.

Folate – Folate is one the B complex vitamins that are so vital for healthy DNA replication and are an essential element in the methylation cycle of cells. Folate and folic acid (vitamin B9) help prevent birth defects in pregnant women and also help in the formation of healthy red blood cells. Folate and folic acid are often confused. Folate is found in natural foods and folic acid is the synthetic form often taken as a supplement. Although they perform a similar function in our cells, folic acid is more stable and bioavailable (usable) than folate. Some individuals have a variation in their methylation (vitamin B) genes, which makes it more difficult to use folate from food sources. In the Chapter 5: Methylation, this process is described in more detail.

Immune system – The immune system is a highly complex biological structure and inter-related system. Inflammation, genetic disorders and immunodeficiencies can result in autoimmune disorders, chronic disease or hormonal disruption. The immune system is a layered defence system designed to protect the body from invading pathogens. The innate immune system and adaptive immune systems depend on the immune system to be able to distinguish between self and non-self molecules. Autoimmunity occurs when the body is no longer able to recognise the difference between self and non-self and cannot respond effectively.

Lutein – Lutein is a member of the antioxidant family of carotenoids. Lutein is very similar to another carotenoid called **zeaxanthin**. Lutein and zeaxanthin are well known for protecting the retina of the eye. Lutein is especially beneficial for age-related macular degeneration and senile cataract formation. Lutein and zeaxanthin are known for their beneficial effects on atherosclerosis and cardiovascular disorders as well.

Lycopene – Lycopene is also a member of the family of **carotenoids**. Lycopene is responsible for the red colouring in tomatoes, red grapefruit and watermelon. Lycopene has a high antioxidant ability and is beneficial for cardiovascular disease prevention as well as anti-aging properties.

Minerals and vitamins are essential micronutrients and act in concert, performing many roles in the human body. Too little or too much of any of these nutrients can upset the delicate balance within our complex human bodies. Although vitamins and minerals are often mentioned together, they are not the same.

Minerals are inorganic, which means they come from either the earth, soil or water and are absorbed by plants. Examples of minerals are calcium, magnesium, potassium, zinc, selenium, iron, chloride, sodium, copper and manganese. Minerals are necessary to maintain the balance of fluid and electrolytes in the body. Minerals are also needed as cofactors for enzyme function. Minerals work to maintain the heart muscle and nervous system and are important in thyroid function and neurological processes as well.

Quercetin – Quercetin is a flavonoid found in many plant foods such as apples, onions, capers and kale. Quercetin-containing foods can be eaten as part of an anti-inflammatory diet.

Vitamins are organic and made by plants or animals. Fat-soluble vitamins include vitamin A, vitamin D, vitamin E and vitamin K. These vitamins are important for eye, skin, lung, bone, gastrointestinal tract and nervous system health.

Water-soluble vitamins include vitamin B complex (folic acid B9, niacin B3, biotin B7, pantothenic acid B5, riboflavin B2, thiamin B1, vitamin B6, vitamin B12) and vitamin C. Vitamin C facilitates energy production and release and is used during methylation and collagen formation.

Acknowledgements

We have lots of people to thank.

Firstly, to Peta Nightingale at Bookouture – what a fortuitous dog walk that was on Wimbledon Common. When she first introduced us to Claire Bord, our editor, we knew that we wanted to be part of the Bookouture family. Claire held our hands every step of the way, encouraging us to share with the world the wonders of nutrigenomics.

Araminta Whitley, our agent, has our best interests at heart and can always be relied on to offer thought-provoking advice.

So many friends have helped us achieve this dream. Dawn Klatzko is a true 'mensch', author and amazing executive and business coach. We spent hours discussing our business with her and she was incredibly generous with her time and unique insights.

Catherine Boardman constantly challenged us to cut back on the scientific jargon and write a book that everyone can understand. Thanks also to Abby, another amazing mate who has tested recipes and walked by our side for over 20 years.

And finally, family. We will miss Grant everyday forever more. This book is for you.

Matthew and his 'bwilliant' kids, Larry, Molly, Rosie and Lottie – thanks for Sunday night suppers 'suffering all that vegetarian food' and discussing what the best chocolate bars are.

Home-cooked food is one of the cornerstones of our family. Here's to a lifetime of family, feasts and fun.

www.ingramcontent.com/pod-product-compliance
Lightning Source LLC
LaVergne TN
LVHW071655060526
838200LV00030B/468